The
Treason
of the
Intellectuals

The
Treason
of the
Intellectuals

Julien Benda
With a new introduction by Roger Kimball

Translated by Richard Aldington

Transaction Publishers
New Brunswick (U.S.A.) and London (U.K.)

Fourth paperback printing 2009
New material this edition copyright © 2007 by Transaction Publishers, New
Brunswick, New Jersey. Originally published in 1928 by William Morrow &
Company, New York.

This book is printed on acid-free paper that meets the American National
Standard for Permanence of Paper for Printed Library Materials.

Library of Congress Catalog Number: 2006050059
ISBN: 978-1-4128-0623-7
Printed in the United States of America

Library of Congress Cataloging-in-Publication Data

Benda, Julien, 1867-1956.
    [Trahison des clercs. English]
    The treason of the intellectuals / Julien Benda ; with a new introduction by
    Roger Kimball ; translated by Richard Aldington.
        p. cm.
    Includes bibliographical references.
    ISBN 1-4128-0623-2 (alk. paper)
    1. Intellectuals. 2. Nationalism. 3. Philosophy. I. Title.

HM213.B44   2006
305.5'—dc22   2006050059

"The world is suffering from lack of faith
in a transcendental truth."

Renouvier.

CONTENTS

INTRODUCTION TO THE TRANSACTION EDITION

THE TREASON OF THE INTELLECTUALS AND "THE UNDOING OF THOUGHT"

"When hatred of culture becomes itself a part of culture, the life of the mind loses all meaning."
—Alain Finkielkraut, The Undoing of Thought

"Today we are trying to spread knowledge everywhere. Who knows if in centuries to come there will not be universities for re-establishing our former ignorance?"
—Georg Christoph Lichtenberg (1742–1799)

I

In 1927, the French essayist Julien Benda published his famous attack on the intellectual corruption of the age, *La Trahison des clercs*. I said "famous," but perhaps "once famous" would have been more accurate. Today, only the title of the book, not its argument, enjoys currency. "La trahison des clercs": it is one of those phrases that bristles with hints and associations without stating anything definite. The book itself, as Jacques Barzun said of Walter Bagehot, is well known without being known well. I hope that this new edition of this neglected classic will change that. *La Trahison des clercs* has never been more pertinent.

Benda tells us that he uses the term "clerc" in "the medieval sense" to mean "scribe"—someone we would now call a member of the intelligentsia, an "intellectual." Academics and journalists, pundits, moralists, and pontificators of all varieties are in this sense clercs. The English translation, *The Treason of the Intellectuals*, sums it up neatly.

The "treason" in question was the betrayal by the "clerks" of their vocation as men devoted to the life of the mind. From the time of the pre-Socratics, intellectuals, considered in this role, had been a breed apart. In Benda's terms, they were understood to be "all those whose activity essentially is not the pursuit of practical aims, all those who seek their joy in the practice of an art or a science or a metaphysical speculation, in short in the possession of non-material advantages." Thanks to such men, Benda wrote, "humanity did evil for two thousand years, but honored good. This contradiction was an honor to the human species, and formed the rift whereby civilization slipped into the world."

According to Benda, however, this situation was changing in the early decades of the twentieth century. More and more, intellectuals were abandoning their attachment to the traditional panoply of philosophical and scholarly ideals. One clear sign of the change was the attack on the Enlightenment ideal of universal humanity and the concomitant glorification of various particularisms. The attack on the universal went forward in social and political life as well as in the refined precincts of epistemology and metaphysics: "Those who for centuries had exhorted men, at least theoretically, to deaden the feeling of their differences . . . have now come to praise them, according to where the sermon is given, for their 'fidelity to the French soul,' 'the immutability of their German consciousness,' for the 'fervor of their Italian hearts.'" In short, intellectuals began to immerse themselves in the unsettlingly practical and material world of political passions: precisely those passions, Benda observed, "owing to which men rise up against other men, the chief of which are racial passions, class passions and national passions." The "rift" into which civilization had been wont to slip narrowed and threatened to close altogether. (It is a significant linguistic-historical fact that the term *intellectuel* entered the language in the 1890s in course of the Dreyfus Affair.)

Writing at a moment when ethnic and nationalistic hatreds were again threatening to tear Europe asunder, Benda's diagnosis assumed the lineaments of a prophecy—one that continues to have deep resonance today. "Our age is indeed the age of the *intellectual organization of political hatreds*," he wrote. "It will be one of its chief claims to notice in the moral history of humanity." There was no need to add that its place in moral history would be as a cautionary tale. In little more than a decade, Benda's prediction that, because of the "great betrayal" of the intellectuals, humanity was "heading for the greatest and most perfect war ever seen in the world," would achieve a terrifying corroboration.

Julien Benda was not so naïve as to believe that intellectuals as a class had ever entirely abstained from political involvement, or, indeed, from involvement in the realm of practical affairs. Nor did he believe that intellectuals, as citizens, necessarily should abstain from political commitment or practical affairs. The "treason" or betrayal he sought to publish concerned the way that intellectuals had lately allowed political commitment to insinuate itself into their understanding of the intellectual vocation as such. Increasingly, Benda claimed, politics was "mingled with their work as artists, as men of learning, as philosophers." The ideal of disinterested judgment and faith in the universality of truth: such traditional guiding principles of intellectual life were more and more contemptuously deployed as masks when they were not jettisoned altogether. Benda castigated this development as the *"desire to abase the values of knowledge before the values of action."*

In its crassest but perhaps also most powerful form, this desire led to that familiar phenomenon Benda dubbed "the cult of success." It is summed up, he writes, in "the teaching that says that when a will is successful that fact alone gives it a moral value, whereas the will which fails is for that reason alone deserving of contempt." In itself, this idea is hardly novel, as history from the Greek sophists on down reminds us. In Plato's *Gorgias*, for instance, the sophist Callicles expresses his contempt for Socrates' devotion to philosophy: "I feel toward philosophers very much as I do toward those who lisp and play the child." Callicles taunts Socrates with the idea that "the more powerful, the better, and the stronger" are simply different words for the same thing. Successfully pursued, he insists, "luxury and intemperance . . . *are* virtue and happiness, and all the rest is tinsel." How contemporary Callicles sounds!

In Benda's formula, this boils down to the conviction that "politics decides morality." To be sure, the cynicism that Callicles espoused is perennial: like the poor, it will be always with us. What Benda found novel was the *accreditation* of such cynicism by intellectuals. "It is true indeed that these new 'clerks' declare that they do not know what is meant by justice, truth, and other 'metaphysical fogs,' that for them the true is determined by the useful, the just by circumstances," he noted. "All these things were taught by Callicles, but with this difference; he revolted all the important thinkers of his time."

In other words, the real treason of the intellectuals was not that they countenanced Callicles but that they championed him. To appreciate the force of Benda's thesis one need only think of that most influential modern Callicles, Friedrich Nietzsche. His doctrine of "the will to power," his contempt for the "slave morality" of Christianity, his plea for an ethic "beyond good and evil," his infatuation with violence—all epitomize the disastrous "pragmatism" that marks the intellectual's "treason." The real problem was not the unattainability but the disintegration of ideals: an event that Nietzsche hailed as the "transvaluation of all values." "Formerly," Benda observed, "leaders of

States practiced realism, but did not honor it; . . . With them morality was violated but moral notions remained intact; *and that is why, in spite of all their violence, they did not disturb civilization."*

Benda understood that the stakes were high: the treason of the intellectuals signaled not simply the corruption of a bunch of scribblers but a fundamental betrayal of culture. By embracing the ethic of Callicles, intellectuals had, Benda reckoned, precipitated "one of the most remarkable turning points in the moral history of the human species." "It is impossible," he continued,

> to exaggerate the importance of a movement whereby those who for twenty centuries taught Man that the criterion of the morality of an act is its disinterestedness, that good is a decree of his reason insofar as it is universal, that his will is only moral if it seeks its law outside its objects, should begin to teach him that the moral act is the act whereby he secures his existence against an environment which disputes it, that his will is moral insofar it is a will "to power," that the part of his soul which determines what is good is its "will to live" wherein it is most "hostile to all reason," that the morality of an act is measured by its adaptation to its end, and that the only morality is the morality of circumstances. The educators of the human mind now take sides with Callicles against Socrates, a revolution which I dare to say seems to me more important than all political upheavals.

II

The Treason of the Intellectuals is an energetic hodgepodge of a book. The philosopher Jean-François Revel described it as "one of the fussiest pleas on behalf of the necessary independence of intellectuals." Certainly it is rich, quirky, erudite, digressive, and polemical: more an exclamation than an analysis. Partisan in its claims for disinterestedness, it is ruthless in its defense of intellectual high-mindedness. Yet given the horrific events that unfolded in the decades following its publication, Benda's unremitting attack on the politicization of the intellect and ethnic separatism cannot but strike us as prescient. And given the continuing echo in our own time of the problems he anatomized, the relevance of his observations to our situation can hardly be doubted. From the savage flowering of ethnic and religious hatreds in the Middle East and throughout Europe to the mendacious demands for political correctness and multiculturalism on college campuses everywhere in the West, the treason of the intellectuals continues to play out its unedifying drama. Benda spoke of "a cataclysm in the moral notions of those who educate the world." That cataclysm is erupting in every corner of cultural life today.

In 1988, the young French philosopher and cultural critic Alain Finkielkraut took up where Benda left off, producing a brief but searching inventory of our contemporary cataclysms. Entitled *La Défaite de la pensée* ("The 'Defeat' or 'Undoing' of Thought"), his essay is in part an updated taxonomy of intellectual betrayals. In this sense, the book is a trahison des clercs for the post-Communist world, a world dominated as much by the leveling imperatives of pop culture as by resurgent nationalism and ethnic separatism. Beginning with Benda, Finkielkraut catalogues several prominent strategies that contemporary intellectuals have employed to retreat from the universal. A frequent point of reference is the eighteenth-century German Romantic philosopher Johann Gottfried Herder. "From the beginning, or to be more precise, from the time of Plato until that of Voltaire," he writes, "human diversity had come before the tribunal of universal values; with Herder the eternal values were condemned by the court of diversity."

Finkielkraut focuses especially on Herder's definitively anti-Enlightenment idea of the *Volksgeist* or "national spirit." Quoting the French historian Ernest Renan, he describes the idea as "the most dangerous explosive of modern times." "Nothing," he writes, "can stop a state that has become prey to the *Volksgeist*." It is one of Finkielkraut's leitmotifs that today's multiculturalists are in many respects Herder's (generally unwitting) heirs. True, Herder's emphasis on history and language did much to temper the tendency to abstraction that one finds in some expressions of the Enlightenment. In his classic book on the philosophy of the Enlightenment, Ernst Cassirer even remarked that "Herder's achievement is one of the greatest intellectual triumphs of the philosophy of the Enlightenment." Nevertheless, the multiculturalists' obsession with "diversity" and ethnic origins is in many ways a contemporary redaction of Herder's elevation of racial particularism over the universalizing mandate of reason.

Finkielkraut opposes this just as the mature Goethe once took issue with Herder's adoration of the *Volksgeist*. Finkielkraut concedes that we all "relate to a particular tradition" and are "shaped by our national identity." But, unlike the multiculturalists, he soberly insists that "this reality merit[s] some recognition, not idolatry." In Goethe's words, "A generalized tolerance will be best achieved if we leave undisturbed whatever it is which constitutes the special character of particular individuals and peoples, whilst at the same time we retain the conviction that the distinctive worth of anything with true merit lies in its belonging to all humanity."

The Undoing of Thought resembles *The Treason of the Intellectuals* stylistically as well as thematically. Both books are sometimes breathless congeries of sources and aperçus. And Finkielkraut, like Benda, tends to proceed more by collage than by demonstration. But he does not simply recapitulate Benda's argument. The geography of intellectual betrayal has changed dramatically in the last seventy-odd years. In 1927, intellectuals still had something definite to betray. In today's "postmodernist" world, the terrain is far mushier: the claims of tradition are much attenuated and betrayal is often only a matter of acquiescence. Finkielkraut's distinctive contribution is to have taken the measure of the cultural swamp that surrounds us, to have delineated the links joining the politicization of the intellect and its current forms of debasement.

In the broadest terms, *The Undoing of Thought* is a brief for the principles of the Enlightenment—not the antinomian Enlightenment that took root in France and made itself the enemy of tradition, but that more modest project promulgated by such British writers as David Hume and Adam Smith. According to this version of Enlightenment, mankind is united by a common humanity that transcends ethnic, racial, and sexual divisions. The humanizing "reason" that Enlightenment champions is a universal reason, sharable, in principle, by all. Such ideals have not fared well in recent decades: Herder's progeny have labored hard to discredit them. Granted, the belief that there is "Jewish thinking" or "Soviet science" or "Aryan art" is no longer as widespread as it once was. But the dispersal of these particular chimeras has provided no inoculation against kindred fabrications: "African knowledge," "female language," "Eurocentric science," "Islamic truth": these are among today's talismanic fetishes.

Then, too, one finds a stunning array of anti-Enlightenment phantasmagoria congregated under the banner of "anti-positivism." The idea that history is a "myth," that the truths of science are merely "fictions" dressed up in forbidding clothes, that reason and language are powerless to discover the truth—more, that truth itself is a deceitful ideological construct: these and other absurdities are now part of the standard intellectual diet of Western intellectuals. The Frankfurt School Marxists Max Horkheimer and

Theodor Adorno gave an exemplary but by no means un-characteristic demonstration of one strain of this brand of anti-rational animus in the mid-1940s. Safely ensconced in Los Angeles, these refugees from Hitler's Reich published an influential essay on the concept of Enlightenment. Among much else, they assured readers that "Enlightenment is to-talitarian." Never mind that at that very moment the Nazi war machine—representing what one might be forgiven for calling *real* totalitarianism—was busy liquidating millions of people in order to fulfill another set of anti-Enlightenment fantasies inspired by devotion to the *Volksgeist.*

III

The diatribe that Horkheimer and Adorno mounted against the concept of Enlightenment reminds us of an important peculiarity about the history of Enlightenment: namely, that it is a movement of thought that began as a reaction against tradition and has now emerged as one of tradition's most important safeguards. Historically, the Enlightenment arose as a deeply anticlerical and, perforce, anti-traditional movement. Its goal, in Kant's famous phrase, was to release man from his "self-imposed im-maturity." The chief enemy of Enlightenment was "su-perstition," an omnibus term that included all manner of religious, philosophical, and moral ideas.

But as the sociologist Edward Shils has noted, although the Enlightenment was in important respects "antithetical to tradition" in its origins, its success was due in large part "to the fact that it was promulgated and pursued in a society in which substantive traditions were rather strong." "It was successful against its enemies," Shils notes in his book *Tradition* (1981),

> because the enemies were strong enough to resist its complete victory over them. Living on a soil of substantive traditionality, the ideas of the Enlightenment advanced without undoing themselves. As long as respect for authority on the one side and self-confidence in those exercising authority on the other persisted, the Enlightenment's ideal of emancipation through the exercise of reason went forward. It did not ravage society as it would have done had society lost all legitimacy.

It is this mature form of Enlightenment, championing reason but respectful of tradition, that Finkielkraut holds up as an ideal.

What Finkielkraut calls "the undoing of thought" flows from the widespread disintegration of a faith. At the center of that faith is the assumption that the life of thought is "the higher life" and that culture—what the Germans call *Bildung*—is its end or goal. The process of disintegration has lately become an explicit attack on culture. This is not simply to say that there are many anti-intellectual elements in society: that has always been the case. "Non-thought," in Finkielkraut's phrase, has always co-existed with the life of the mind. The innovation of contemporary culture is to have obliterated the distinction between the two. "It is," he writes, "the first time in European history that non-thought has donned the same label and enjoyed the same status as thought itself, and the first time that those who, in the name of 'high culture,' dare to call this non-thought by its name, are dismissed as racists and reactionaries." The attack is perpetrated not from outside, by uncomprehending barbarians, but chiefly from inside, by a new class of barbarians, the self-made barbarians of the intelligentsia. This is the undoing of thought. This is the new "treason of the intellectuals."

There are many sides to this phenomenon. What Finkielkraut has given us is not a systematic dissection but a kind of pathologist's scrapbook. He reminds us, for example, that the multiculturalists' demand for "diversity" requires the eclipse of the individual in favor of the group. "Their most extraordinary feat," he observes, "is to have put forward as the ultimate individual liberty the unconditional primacy of the collective." Western rationalism and individualism are rejected in the name of a more "authentic" cult.

One example: Finkielkraut quotes a champion of multiculturalism who maintains that "to help immigrants means first of all respecting them for what they are, respecting whatever they aspire to in their national life, in their distinctive culture and in their attachment to their spiritual and religious roots." Would this, Finkielkraut asks, include "respecting" those religious codes which demanded that the barren woman be cast out and the adultress be punished with death? What about those cultures in which the testimony of one man counts for that of two women? In which female circumcision is practiced? In which slavery flourishes? In which mixed marriages are forbidden and polygamy encouraged? Multiculturalism, as Finkielkraut points out, requires that we respect such practices. To criticize them is to be dismissed as "racist" and "ethnocentric." In this secular age, "cultural identity" steps in where the transcendent once was: "Fanaticism is indefensible when it appeals to heaven, but beyond reproach when it is grounded in antiquity and cultural distinctiveness."

To a large extent, the abdication of reason demanded by multiculturalism has been the result of what we might call the subjection of culture to anthropology. Finkielkraut speaks in this context of a "cheerful confusion which raises everyday anthropological practices to the pinnacle of the human race's greatest achievements." This process began in the nineteenth century, but it has been greatly accelerated in our own age. One thinks, for example, of the tireless campaigning of that great anthropological leveler, Claude Lévi-Strauss. Lévi-Strauss is assuredly a brilliant writer; but he was an extraordinarily baneful influence. Already in the early 1950s, when he was pontificating for UNESCO, he was urging all and sundry to "fight against ranking cultural differences hierarchically." In *La Pensée sauvage* (1961), he warned against the "false antinomy between logical and prelogical mentality" and was careful in his descriptions of natives to refer to "so-called primitive thought." "So-called" indeed.

In a famous article on race and history, Lévi-Strauss maintained that the barbarian was not the opposite of the civilized man but "first of all the man who believes there is such a thing as barbarism." That of course is good to know. It helps one to appreciate Lévi-Strauss's claim, in *Tristes Tropiques* (1955), that the "true purpose of civilization" is to produce "inertia." As one ruminates on the proposition that cultures should not be ranked hierarchically, it is also well to consider what Lévi-Strauss coyly refers to as "the positive forms of cannibalism." For Lévi-Strauss, cannibalism has been unfairly stigmatized in the "so-called" civilized West. In fact, he explains, cannibalism was "often observed with great discretion, the vital mouthful being made up of a small quantity of organic matter mixed, on occasion, with other forms of food." What, merely a "vital mouthful"? Not to worry! Only an ignoramus who believed that there were important distinctions, *qualitative* distinctions, between the barbarian and the civilized man could possibly think of objecting.

Of course, the attack on distinctions that Finkielkraut castigates takes place not only among cultures but also within a given culture. Here again, the anthropological imperative has played a major role. "Under the equalizing eye of social science," he writes,

> hierarchies are abolished, and all the criteria of taste are exposed as arbitrary. From now on no rigid division separates masterpieces from run-of-the-mill works. The same fundamental structure, the same

general and elemental traits are common to the "great" novels (whose
excellence will henceforth be demystified by the accompanying quotation marks) and plebian types of narrative activity.

For confirmation of this, one need only glance at the
pronouncements of our critics. Whether working in the
academy or other cultural institutions, they bring us the
same news: there is "no such thing" as intrinsic merit;
"quality" is only an ideological construction; aesthetic value
is a distillation of social power; etc., etc.

In describing this process of leveling, Finkielkraut distinguishes between those who wish to obliterate distinctions in the name of politics and those who do so out of a
kind of narcissism. The multiculturalists wave the standard
of radical politics and say (in the words of a nineteenth-
century Russian populist slogan that Finkielkraut quotes):
"A pair of boots is worth more than Shakespeare." Those
whom Finkielkraut calls "postmodernists," waving the
standard of radical chic, declare that Shakespeare is no better than the latest fashion—no better, say, than the newest
item offered by Calvin Klein. The litany that Finkielkraut
recites is familiar:

> A comic which combines exciting intrigue and some pretty pictures is
> just as good as a Nabokov novel. What little Lolitas read is as good as
> *Lolita*. An effective publicity slogan counts for as much as a poem by
> Apollinaire or Francis Ponge.... The footballer and the choreographer,
> the painter and the couturier, the writer and the ad-man, the musician
> and the rock-and-roller, are all the same: creators. We must scrap the
> prejudice which restricts that title to certain people and regards others
> as sub-cultural.

The upshot is not only that Shakespeare is downgraded, but also that the bootmaker is elevated. "It is not just that high culture must be demystified; sport, fashion and leisure now lay claim to high cultural status." A grotesque fantasy? Anyone who thinks so should take a moment to recall the major exhibition called "High & Low: Modern Art and Popular Culture" that the Museum of Modern Art mounted in the 1990s: it might have been called "Krazy Kat Meets Picasso." Few events can have so consummately summed up the corrosive trivialization of culture now perpetrated by those entrusted with preserving it. Among other things, that exhibition demonstrated the extent to which the apotheosis of popular culture undermines the very possibility of appreciating high art on its own terms. When the distinction between culture and entertainment is obliterated, high art is orphaned, exiled from the only context in which its distinctive meaning can manifest itself: Picasso *becomes* a kind of cartoon. This, more than any elitism or obscurity, is the real threat to culture today. As Hannah Arendt once observed, "there are many great authors of the past who have survived centuries of oblivion and neglect, but it is still an open question whether they will be able to survive an entertaining version of what they have to say."

IV

And this brings us to the question of freedom. Finkielkraut notes that the rhetoric of postmodernism is in some ways similar to the rhetoric of Enlightenment. Both look forward to releasing man from his "self-imposed immaturity." But there is this difference: Enlightenment looks to culture as a repository of values that transcend the self, postmodernism looks to the fleeting desires of the isolated self as the only legitimate source of value. Questions of "lifestyle" (ominous neologism!) come to occupy the place once inhabited by moral convictions and intellectual principles. For the postmodernist, then, "culture is no longer seen as a means of emancipation, but as one of the élitist obstacles to this." The postmodernist regards the products of culture as valuable only to the extent that they are sources of amusement or distraction. In order to realize the freedom that postmodernism promises—freedom understood as the emancipation from values that transcend the self—culture must be transformed into a field of arbitrary "options." "The post-modern individual," Finkielkraut writes, "is a free and easy bundle of fleeting and contingent appetites. He has forgotten that liberty involves more than the ability to change one's chains, and that culture itself is more than a satiated whim."

What Finkielkraut has understood with admirable clarity is that modern attacks on elitism represent not the extension but the destruction of culture. "Democracy," he writes, "once implied access to culture for everybody. From now on it is going to mean everyone's right to the culture of his choice." This may sound marvelous—it is after all the slogan one hears shouted in academic and cultural institutions across the country—but the result is precisely the opposite of what was intended. "'All cultures are equally legitimate and everything is cultural,' is the common cry of affluent society's spoiled children and of the detractors of the West." The irony, alas, is that by removing standards and declaring that "anything goes," one does not get more culture, one gets more and more debased imitations of culture. This fraud is the dirty secret that our cultural commissars refuse to acknowledge.

There is another, perhaps even darker, result of the undoing of thought. The disintegration of faith in reason and common humanity leads not only to a destruction of standards, but also involves a crisis of courage. "A careless indifference to grand causes," Finkielkraut warns, "has its counterpart in abdication in the face of force." As the impassioned proponents of "diversity" meet the postmodern apostles of acquiescence, fanaticism mixes with apathy to challenge the commitment required to preserve freedom. Communism may have been effectively discredited. But "what is dying along with it . . . is not the totalitarian cast of mind, but the idea of a world common to all men." Julien Benda took his epigraph for *La Trahison des clercs* from the nineteenth-century French philosopher Charles Renouvier: *Le monde souffre du manque de foi en une vérité transcendante:* "The world suffers from lack of faith in a transcendent truth." Without some such faith, we are powerless against the depredations of intellectuals who have embraced the nihilism of Callicles as their truth.

Roger Kimball

THE *title of* M. *Benda's book is* La Trahison des Clercs. *The word "Clercs," which occurs throughout the book, is defined by* M. *Benda's as "all those who speak to the world in a transcendental manner." I do not know the English word for "all those who speak to the world in a transcendental manner." But in Chaucer's time the word "clerk" ("a clerke of Oxenforde") meant any one who was not a "layman," a word employed by* M. *Benda as the antithesis to "clerk." We still use the word in this sense when we speak of a "clerk in holy orders" and retain its root in "cleric." A "cleric" is the person described by* M. *Benda as "preëminently a clerk." If the words "in holy orders" are subtracted from "a clerk in holy orders," the remaining "clerk" is roughly what* M. *Benda means, though he also uses "clerk" to include "a clerk in holy orders." Nowadays a clerk is a person who performs sedentary labor in an office, and the word in England is pronounced "clark." In America a clerk (pronounced "clurrk") is what the English call a shop-assistant. In order to avoid a misleading title I have called this translation* The Treason of the Intellectuals, *giving* M. *Benda's title in brackets afterwards. Where the word "clerk" first occurs in the book, I have added the words "in the* medieval sense," and throughout the text I have invariably written the word in inverted commas, "clerk," to avoid any possible misunderstanding.

I should add that the words "real" and "realism" are nearly always used in this book as the antithesis to "ideal" and "idealism." Other abstract words are used in a rather special sense which I hope will be plain from the context.

R. A.

TOLSTOI relates that when he was in the Army he saw one of his brother officers strike a man who fell out from the ranks during a march. Tolstoi said to him:—

"Are you not ashamed to treat a fellow human being in this way? Have you not read the Gospels?"

The other officer replied:—

"And have you not read Army Orders?"

This retort will always be thrown back at the spiritual man who tries to take the direction of the material. To me it seems a very wise one. Those who lead men to the conquest of material things have no need of justice and charity.

Nevertheless I think it important that there should be men—even if they are scorned—who urge their fellow beings to other religions than the religion of the material. Now, those who should play this part (to whom I have given the name of "clerks" in the medieval sense of the word) have not only ceased to do so, but are playing an exactly contrary part. Most of the influential moralists of the past fifty years in Europe, particularly the men of letters in France, call upon mankind to sneer at the Gospel and to read Army Orders.

This new teaching seems to me all the more deserving of serious attention because it is addressed to a humanity which of its own volition is now established in materialism with a decisiveness hitherto unknown. And I shall begin by showing this to be true.

I — THE MODERN PERFECTING OF POLITICAL PASSIONS

I.

WE ARE TO CONSIDER those passions termed political, owing to which men rise up against other men,
the chief of which are racial passions, class passions
and national passions. Those persons who are most
determined to believe in the inevitable progress of
the human species, especially in its indispensable
movement towards more peace and love, cannot
deny that during the past century these passions
have attained—and day by day increasingly so—in
several most important directions, a degree of perfection hitherto unknown in history.

In the first place they affect a large number of
men they never before affected. When, for example, we study the civil wars which convulsed
France in the sixteenth century, and even those at
the end of the eighteenth century, we are struck
by the small number of persons whose minds were
really disturbed by these events. While history, up
to the nineteenth century, is filled with long European wars which left the great majority of people
completely indifferent, apart from the material
losses they themselves suffered,[1] it may be said that
to-day there is scarcely a mind in Europe which is
not affected—or thinks itself affected—by a racial
or class or national passion, and most often by

[1] See Note A at the end of this book.

3

all three. The same progress seems to have taken place in the New World, while immense bodies of men in the Far East, who seemed to be free from these impulses, are awakening to social hatred, the party system, and the national spirit insofar as it implies the will to humiliate other men. To-day political passions have attained a *universality* never before known.

They have also attained *coherence*. Thanks to the progress of communication and, still more, to the group spirit, it is clear that the holders of the same political hatred now form a compact impassioned mass, every individual of which feels himself in touch with the infinite numbers of others, whereas a century ago such people were comparatively out of touch with each other and hated in a "scattered" way. This is singularly striking with respect to the working classes who, even in the middle of the nineteenth century, felt only a scattered hostility for the opposing class, attempted only dispersed efforts at war (such as striking in one town, or one union), whereas to-day they form a closely-woven fabric of hatred from one end of Europe to the other. It may be asserted that these coherences will tend to develop still further, for the will to group is one of the most profound characteristics of the modern world, which even in the most unexpected domains (for instance, the domain of thought) is more and more becoming

4

the world of leagues, of "unions" and of "groups."
Is it necessary to say that the passion of the individual is strengthened by feeling itself in prox-
imity to these thousands of similar passions? Let
me add that the individual bestows a mystic personality on the association of which he feels himself a member, and gives it a religious adoration,
which is simply the deification of his own passion,
and no small stimulus to its intensity.

The coherence just described might be called a
surface coherence, but there is added to it a
coherence of essence. For the very reason that the
holders of the same political passion form a more
compact, impassioned group, they also form a more
homogeneous, impassioned group, in which individual ways of feeling disappear and the zeal of
each member more and more takes on the color of
the others. In France, for instance, one cannot but
be struck by the fact that the enemies of the
democratic system (I am speaking of the mass, not
the highest points) display a passion which has little
variety, shows very slight differences in different
persons. How little this mass of hatred is weakened
by personal and original manners of hating—one
might almost say that this passion itself is obedient
to "democratic leveling down"! How much more
uniformity is shown now than a hundred years ago
by the emotions known as anti-semitism, anti-
Clericalism and Socialism, in spite of the immense

number of varieties in the last-named! And do not those who are subject to these emotions now all tend *to say the same thing?* Political passions, as passions, seem to have attained the habit of discipline; they seem to obey a word of command even in the manner they are felt. It is easy to see what increase of strength they acquire thereby.

With some of these passions the increase in homogeneousness is accompanied by an increased *precision.* For instance, we all know that a hundred years ago Socialism was a strong but vague passion with the great mass of its supporters. But to-day Socialism has more closely defined the object it wishes to attain, has determined the exact point where it means to strike its adversary and the movement it intends to create in order to succeed. The same progress may be observed in the anti-democratic movement. And we all know that hatred becomes stronger by becoming more precise.

There is another sort of perfecting of political passions. Throughout history until our own days I see these passions acting intermittently, blazing up and then subsiding. I see that the undoubtedly terrible and numerous explosions of class and race hatred were followed by long periods of calm, or at least of somnolence. Wars between nations lasted for years, but not hatred—even if we may say that it existed. To-day we have only to look every morning at any daily paper and we shall see that

6

political hatreds do not cease for a single day. At best some of them are silent a moment for the benefit of one among them which suddenly claims all the subject's strength. This is the period of "national unions," which do not in the very least herald in the reign of love, but merely of a general hatred which for the moment dominates partial hatreds. To-day political passions have acquired *continuity*, which is so rare a quality in all feelings.

Let us consider a moment the impulse which causes partial hatreds to abdicate in favor of another, more general hatred, which derives a new religion of itself and hence a new strength, from the feeling of its generality. Perhaps it has not been sufficiently observed that this sort of impulse is one of the essential characteristics of the nineteenth century. Twice during the nineteenth century, in Germany and in Italy, the age-old hatreds of petty States disappeared in favor of a great national passion. In the same period (more precisely, at the end of the eighteenth century) in France, the mutual hatred of the Court nobles and the country nobles was extinguished in the greater hatred of both parties for all who were not nobles; the hatred between the military and legal nobles disappeared in the same impulse; the hatred between the upper and lower ranks of the clergy vanished in their common hatred of laicality; the hatred between clergy and nobility expired to the

7

profit of their mutual hatred for the commons. And in our times the hatred between the three orders has melted into one hatred, that of the possessing classes for the working class. The condensation of political passions into a small number of very simple hatreds, springing from the deepest roots of the human heart, is a conquest of modern times.[1]

I also believe that I see a great progress in political passions to-day in their relation to other passions in the same person. Political passions undoubtedly occupied more of the attention of a bourgeois of ancient France than is usually supposed, but less than the love of money and pleasure, family feeling and the calls of vanity; while the least we can say of his modern equivalent is that when political passions take possession of him, they do so to the same extent as the other passions. Compare, for instance, the tiny place occupied by political passions in the French bourgeois as he appears in the Fabliaux, in medieval drama, the novels of Scarron, Furetière and Charles Sorel,[2] with the same bourgeois as drawn by Balzac, Stendhal, Anatole France,

---

[1] It is to be noted that a little more than a century ago French working men from different provinces frequently engaged in desperate fights among themselves. (See Martin Nadaud, *Mémoires de Léonard*, p. 93.)

[2] See Petit de Julleville, *La Comédie et les Mœurs en France au moyen age*, and André Le Breton, *Le Roman au XVIIe Siècle.*

Abel Hermant and Paul Bourget. (Of course, I am not speaking of times of crisis, like the Ligue and the Fronde, when political passions occupied the whole individual as soon as they touched him at all.) The truth is that to-day political passions are invading most of the other passions in the bourgeoisie, and weakening the latter to their own profit. Every one knows that in our own days family rivalries, commercial enmities, ambitions and the competition for public honors are all tainted with political passion. An apostle of the modern mind clamors for "politics first." He might have observed that nowadays it is politics everywhere, politics always and nothing but politics.[1] We have only to open our eyes to see when an increase of power is acquired by political passion when combined with other passions, so numerous, so constant and so strong themselves. Coming to the man of the people, we can measure the increase of his political passions in relation to his other passions in modern times by considering, as Stendhal puts it, how long his whole passion was limited to wishing (*a*) Not to be killed, (*b*) For a good warm coat.

---

[1] The great novelty is that to-day people accept the position that everything should be political, that they should proclaim it and take a pride in it. Otherwise it is perfectly obvious that men, shopkeepers, or poets, have not waited for the present time to try to get rid of a rival by political means. Remember how La Fontaine's rivals kept him out of the Académie for ten years.

9

And then we may recollect that when a little less misery permitted him a few general ideas, how long it was before his vague desire for social changes was transformed into a passion, i.e. showing the two essential characteristics of passion: The fixed idea, and the need to put it into action.[1] I think it may be said that political passions in all classes to-day have attained a degree of *preponderance over all other passions* in those affected such as hitherto had been unknown.

The reader will already have perceived an all-important factor in the impulses I have been describing. Political passions rendered universal, coherent, homogeneous, permanent, preponderant —every one can recognize there to a great extent the work of the cheap daily political newspaper. One cannot help reflecting and wondering whether it may not be that inter-human wars are only just beginning, when one thinks of this instrument for developing their own passions which men have just invented, or at least brought to a degree of power never seen before, to which they abandon themselves with all the expansion of their hearts every morning as soon as they are awake.

I have now showed what might be called the

---

[1] As de Tocqueville profoundly remarks, these only occurred when a first improvement in his condition encouraged the man of the people to want more; i.e. towards the end of the eighteenth century.

perfecting of political passions on the surface, in their more or less exterior aspects. But they have also become strangely perfected in depth and inner strength.

In the first place they have made an immense advance in consciousness of themselves. Here again, largely owing to the influence of the newspaper, it is clear that the mind affected by political hatred to-day becomes conscious of its own passion, formulates it, sees it, with an accuracy unknown to the same sort of mind fifty years ago. There is no need to say how much the passion is intensified by this. And while I am on this subject I should like to point to two passions, which have certainly not come to birth in our times but have attained consciousness of themselves, self-assertion, a pride in themselves.

The first is what I shall call a certain *Jewish nationalism*. In the past, when the Jews were accused in various countries of forming an inferior race, or at any rate a peculiar people not to be assimilated, they replied by denying their peculiarity, by trying to get rid of all appearance of peculiarity, and by refusing to admit the reality of race. But in the last few years we see some of them laboring to assert this peculiarity, to define its characteristics—or what they think such—taking a pride in it, and condemning every effort at assimilation with their opponents (see the works of Israel Zangwill, of

André Spire, and the *Revue Juive*). Here I am not trying to discover whether the impulse of these Jews is or is not nobler than the efforts of so many others to have their origin pardoned them; I am simply pointing out to those interested in the progress of peace in the world that our age has added one more arrogance to those which set men against each other, at least to the extent that it is conscious and proud of itself.[1]

The other impulse I am thinking of is *"bourgeoisism,"* by which I mean the passion of the bourgeois class in asserting itself against the class by which it is threatened. It may be said that until our own times, "class hatred," as a conscious hatred proud of itself, was chiefly the hatred of the laborer for the bourgeois. The reciprocal hatred was much less clearly confessed. Ashamed of an egotism they thought peculiar to their own caste, the bourgeois temporized with this egotism, would not admit even to themselves that it existed, tried to convince themselves and others that it was a form of interest in the common good.[2] The bourgeois replied to the dogma of the class war by denying that there really

---

[1] I am here speaking of Western Jews of the bourgeois class. The Jewish proletariat did not await our time to plunge into the feeling of its racial peculiarity. However, it does so without giving provocation.

[2] This was the notion expressed by Benedict XV when he told the poor "to take delight in the prosperity of elevated persons and to expect confidently their assistance."

are any classes, thereby showing that while they felt an inalterable opposition to the adverse party, they were unwilling to admit that they felt it. To-day we have only to think of Italian "Fascism," of a certain "Eloge du Bourgeois Français," and numerous other manifestations of the same kind,[1] and we shall see that the bourgeoisie are becoming fully conscious of their specific egotisms, are proclaiming and venerating them as such and as though these egotisms were bound up with the supreme interests of the human race, that they are proud of this veneration and of setting up these egotisms against those which are trying to destroy the bourgeoisie. In our time there has been created the "mysticism" of bourgeois passion in its opposition to the passions of the other class.[2] Here again our age enters in the balance-sheet of humanity the arrival of yet one more passion at full possession of itself.

The progress of political passions in depth dur-

[1] For example, M. Paul Bourget's *La Barricade*, where the author, a disciple of Georges Sorel, exhorts the bourgeoise not to leave to the proletariat the monopoly of class passion and violence. See also André Beaunier, *Les Devoirs de la Violence* (quoted by Halperine-Kaminski in the preface to Tolstoi's book, *The Law of Love and the Law of Violence*).

[2] "The phrase, *the sublime bourgeois*, which would have caused so much laughter twenty years ago, has now acquired for the French bourgeoisie a mystic plenitude owing to its fusion with the highest social and national values." (*Eloge du Bourgeois Français*, p. 284.)

13

ing the past century seems to me most remarkable in the case of national passions.

First of all, owing to the fact that they are experienced to-day by large masses of men, these passions have become *far more purely passionate*. When the national feeling was practically confined to Kings or their Ministers, it consisted chiefly in attachment to some *interest* (desire for territorial expansion, search for commercial advantages and profitable alliances), whereas to-day when this national feeling is continually experienced by common minds, it consists chiefly in the exercise of *pride*. Every one will agree that nationalist passion in the modern citizen is far less founded on a comprehensive knowledge of the national interests (he has an imperfect perception of these interests, he lacks the information necessary and does not try to acquire it, for he is indifferent to questions of foreign policy) than on the pride he feels in his nation, on his will to feel himself one with the nation, to react to the honors and insults he thinks are bestowed on it. No doubt he wants his nation to acquire territories, to be prosperous and to have powerful allies; but he wants all this far less on account of the material results which will accrue to the nation (how much is he conscious of these results?) than on account of the glory, the prestige which the nation will acquire. By becoming popular, national feeling has become

national pride, national susceptibility.[1] To measure how much more purely passionate it has become, how much more perfectly irrational (and
therefore stronger) one has only to think of Jingo-
ism, the form of patriotism specially invented by
democracies. If, in accordance with current opinion, you think that pride is a weaker passion than
self-interest, you may be convinced to the contrary
by observing how commonly men let themselves
be killed on account of a wound to their pride, and
how infrequently for some infraction of their
interests.

[1] Let me define more precisely what is new here. In the
seventeenth century the citizen already had the notion of
national honor; Racine's Letters would be sufficient to prove
it (see a significant page in the *Mémoires* of de Pontis, Book
XIV); but he left it to the King to decide what this honor
demanded; indignation like Vauban's against the peace of
Ryswick "which dishonours the King and the whole nation,"
is a very exceptional emotion under the old *régime*. The
modern citizen claims to feel for himself what is demanded by
the national honor, and he is ready to rise up against his
leaders if they have a different conception of it. This new
development is not peculiar to the nations living under democratic systems; in 1911 the citizens of the German monarchy
thought that the concessions made to their country by France
in exchange for German abstention in Morocco were insufficient, and they were extremely angry with their Sovereign
who had accepted these conditions which, in their opinion,
were an insult to German honor. It may be asserted that the
same thing would be true of France if she ever became a
monarchy again and if the King took it upon himself to feel
the interest of national honor in a different manner to his
subjects. Moreover, this actually happened throughout the
reign of Louis-Philippe.

The susceptibility developed by national sentiment as it has become popular makes the possibility
of wars far greater to-day than in the past. Obviously, with the peoples and with the aptitude of
these new "sovereigns" to rise up in a rage as soon
as they think they are insulted, peace runs an additional danger which did not exist when it depended
only upon Kings and their Ministers, who were far
more purely practical persons, fully self-controlled,
and quite willing to put up with insults when they
did not think themselves the stronger party.[1]
And, in fact, how many times during the last hundred years has the world almost flamed up in war
solely because some nation thought its honor had
been wounded?[2] To this must be added the fact

[1] For example, the humiliation of Olmüts in 1805. It may
be asserted that no democracy would have endured it, at least
with the philosophy displayed by the King of Prussia and his
government. On the other hand, is it necessary to stress the
other dangers to peace which existed under the Kings? It is
sufficient to quote Montesquieu's remark: "The spirit of the
Monarchy is war and aggrandisement."

[2] In 1886, the Schnœbele affair; in 1890, the incident in
Paris where the King of Spain in the uniform of a Colonel of
Uhlans was hooted; in 1891, the incident of the Empress of
Germany passing through Paris; in 1897, Fashoda; in 1904,
the incident of the British trawlers sunk by the Russian Fleet,
etc. Of course, I do not claim that the Kings only waged
practical wars, although with them the allegation of
"wounded honor" was very often a mere pretext. Louis XIV
obviously did not make war on Holland because the Dutch
struck a medal insulting him. Moreover, I shall grant that
from time to time the Kings indulged in military invasions, a
type of elegance which appears to be less and less tempting to

that this national susceptibility provides the leaders of nations with a new and most effective method of starting the wars they need, whether it is employed at home or abroad. They have not failed to see this, which is amply proved by the example of Bismarck and the means by which he provoked war with Austria and with France. From this point of view it seems to me quite correct to say with the French monarchists that "democracy is war," provided that by democracy is meant the attainment of national susceptibility by the masses, and provided that it is recognized that no change in the system of government would destroy this phenomenon.[1]

Another considerable deepening of national passions comes from the fact that the nations are now

the democracies; one cannot now imagine the peace of the world disturbed by excursions like those of Charles VIII into Italy or Charles XII into the Ukraine.

[1] Is it necessary to point out that wars started by public passion against the will of the government have often occurred under monarchies? And not only under constitutional monarchies, like the war of France with Spain in 1823 and with Turkey in 1826, but under absolute monarchies. For instance, the War of the Austrian Succession imposed on Fleury by an uprising of public opinion; the War of American Independence under Louis XVI; in 1806 the war of Prussia against Napoleon. In 1813 the war of Saxony. It seems probable that in 1914 war was imposed on absolute sovereigns like Nicholas II and Wilhelm II by popular passions which they had been exciting for years and then found themselves unable to restrain.

conscious of themselves not only as regards their material existence, their military power, their territorial possessions, and their economic wealth, but as regards their *moral* existence. With a hitherto unknown consciousness (prodigiously fanned by authors) every nation now hugs itself and sets itself up against all other nations as superior in language, art, literature, philosophy, civilization, "culture." Patriotism to-day is the assertion of one form of mind against other forms of mind.[1] We know how much this passion increases its inner strength in this way and that the wars it determines are fiercer than those waged by the Kings, who merely desired the same piece of territory. The prophecy of the old Saxon bard is completely fulfilled: "In those days countries will be something they have not yet become—they will be persons.

[1] "But what is much more important than material facts is the soul of nations. Among all races a kind of effervescence is to be noticed; some defend certain principles, others the opposing principles. By becoming members of the League of Nations, the different peoples do not abandon their *national morality*." (Speech of the German Minister for Foreign Affairs at Geneva, on the occasion of the entry of Germany into the League of Nations, 10th September, 1926.) The orator went on: "Yet this should not result in raising up nation against nation." One is surprised that he did not add: "On the contrary." How much nobler, and at the same time more respectful of the truth, is the language of Treitschke: "This consciousness of themselves which the nations are acquiring and which can only be strengthened by culture, this consciousness means that war will never disappear from the earth, in spite of the closer linking up of interests, in spite of

18

They will feel hatred, and these hatreds will cause wars more terrible than any that have yet been seen." [1]

It is impossible to over-stress the novelty of this form of patriotism in history. It is obviously bound up with the adoption of this passion by the masses of the populace, and seems to have been inaugurated in 1813 by Germany, who is apparently the real teacher of humanity in the matter of democratic patriotism, if by this word is meant the determination of a nation to oppose others in the name of its most fundamental characteristics. [2] (The France of the Revolution and the Empire never dreamed of setting itself up against other nations in the name of its language or of its literature.) This form of patriotism was so little known to preceding ages that there are countless examples

the growing uniformity of customs and the exterior forms of life." (Quoted by Charles Andler in *Les Origines du Pangermanisme*, p. 223.)

[1] This is what Mirabeau seems to have foreseen when he announced to the Constituent Assembly that the wars of the "free nations" would cause the wars of the Kings to be regretted.

[2] The religion of the "national soul" is obviously and logically an emanation of the popular soul. Moreover, it has been sung by an eminently democratic literature: Romanticism. It is to be observed that the worst enemies of Romanticism and of Democracy have adopted it; it is constantly to be found in the Action Française. To such an extent is it now impossible to be a patriot without flattering democratic passions.

of nations adopting the cultures of other nations, even of those with whom they were at war, and in addition reverencing the culture adopted. Shall I refer to the profound respect of Rome for the genius of Greece, though Rome had felt it necessary to crush Greece politically? To the respect of the conquerors of Rome, such as Ataulf and Theodoric, for Roman genius? And, nearer to ourselves, shall I mention Louis XIV annexing Alsace and not for one moment thinking of forbidding the German language? [1]   In the past, nations displayed their sympathy for the culture of other nations with whom they were at war, or invited them to adopt their own. The Duke of Alba took measures to protect the learned men in the towns of Holland, against which he was directing his army; in the eighteenth century, the small German States, allied with Frederick the Great against the French, adopted more freely than ever French ideas, French fashions, French [2] literature; in the midst of the struggle with England, the Convention sent a deputation there to urge the English to adopt the French metric system. [3] The notion that political warfare involves a war of cultures is entirely an invention of modern times, and confers upon them a conspicuous place in the moral history of humanity.

[1] See Note B at the end of the book.
[2] See Brunot, *Histoire de la Langue Française*, t. v, liv. iii.
[3] On this topic see some excellent remarks of Auguste Comte, *Cours de Philosophie Positive*, 57e lecon.

Another strengthening of national passions comes from the determination of the peoples to be conscious of *their past*, more precisely to be conscious of their ambitions as going back to their ancestors, and to vibrate with "centuries-old" aspirations, with attachments to "historical" rights. This Romantic patriotism is also a characteristic of patriotism as practiced by popular minds (by "popular" I here mean all minds governed by the imagination, that is, in the first place, society people and men of letters). I have an idea that when Hugues de Lionne desired for the nation the conquest of Flanders or when Siéyes wanted the Low Countries, they did not think they felt the soul of ancient Gauls reviving in them, any more than Bismarck thought (I am not talking of what he said) of reviving the Teutonic Knights when he coveted the Danish Duchies.[1]

Those who wish to estimate the increase of violence given to national passion by this solemnizing of its desires have only to observe what has happened to this feeling among the Germans, with their claim to be carrying on the spirit of the Holy Roman Empire, and among the Italians since they

---

[1] As a matter of fact, the peoples do not believe either that their ambitions go back to their ancestors; they are ignorant of history and do not believe it to be so even when it is true; they believe they believe, or, more exactly, they want to believe that they believe. However, that is enough to make them ferocious, perhaps more so than if they really believed it.

have set up their aspirations as the revival of those of the Roman Empire.[1] There once again the leaders of the State find in popular sentimentality a new and excellent instrument for carrying out their practical designs, an instrument they well know how to use. To mention only one recent example—think of the result the Italian government was able to obtain from the amazing aptitude of its compatriots to wake up one fine morning and discover that the claim to Fiume was a "centuries-old" claim.

Speaking generally, it may be said that national passions, owing to the fact that they are now exerted by plebeian minds, assume the character of *mysticism*, of a religious adoration almost unknown in these passions in the practical minds of the great nobles. It is unnecessary to add that this makes these passions deeper and stronger. Here once more this plebeian form of patriotism is adopted by all who practice this passion, even when they are the noisiest champions of the aristocracy of the mind. M. Maurras talks of the "goddess France," just as Victor Hugo does. Let me add that this mystical adoration of the nation is not only to be explained by the nature of those who adore, but also by the changes which have taken place in the adored ob-

---

[1] France is here in a position of manifest inferiority in regard to her neighbors. The modern French feel very slight inclinations to claim that they reincarnate the ambitions of Charlemagne or even of Louis XIV, despite the proclamations of certain men of letters.

ject. There is first of all the spectacle of the military force and organization of modern States, which is something far more imposing than of old. And when these States are seen to make war for an indefinite period after they have no more men, and go on subsisting for long years after they have no more money, it is easy to understand why a man who has some tincture of religion in his mind may be led to believe that these States are of an essence different from that of ordinary natural beings.

I shall point out another great increase of power in national sentiment which has occurred in the last half-century. I mean that several very powerful political passions, which were originally independent of nationalist feeling, have now become incorporated with it. These passions are: (a) The movement against the Jews; (b) the movement of the possessing classes against the proletariat; (c) the movement of the champions of authority against the democrats. To-day each one of these passions is identified with national feeling and declares that its adversary implies the negation of nationalism. I may add that when a person is affected by one of these passions he is generally affected by all three; consequently nationalist passion is usually swelled by the addition of all three. Moreover this increase is reciprocal, and it may be said that to-day capitalism, anti-semitism and the party of authority have all received new strength from their union with nationalism. (For additional proof of the strength of these unions, see Note C at the end of this book.)

I cannot drop the subject of the modern perfecting of political passions without mentioning one more characteristic: In all nations the number of persons who feel a direct interest in belonging to a powerful nation is incomparably greater now than in the past. In all the great States to-day I observe that not only the world of industry and big business but a considerable number of small tradesmen, small bourgeois, doctors, lawyers, and even writers and artists, and working men too, feel that for the sake of the prosperity of their own occupations it is essential for them to belong to a powerful group which can make itself feared. Those who are in a position to give an opinion on this sort of change agree that the feeling did not exist, at least in the same clearly defined way as to-day, thirty years ago among the small tradesmen of France, for instance. It seems an even newer thing among the men who belong to the so-called liberal professions; it is certainly something new to hear artists constantly girding at the government of their country because it "does not give the nation enough prestige to impose their art on foreigners." The feeling that from a professional point of view they have an interest in belonging to a powerful nation is also very recent among the working classes. The party of "Nationalist Socialists," which seems to exist everywhere except in France, is a quite modern political development. Among the masters of industry the new development is, not that they feel how much it is to their interest that their nation should be powerful, but that the feeling is to-day transformed into action, into formal pressure on their governments.[1] This extension of patriotism based on interest certainly does not prevent this sort of patriotism (as I said above) from being much less wide-spread than the patriotism[2] based on pride; nevertheless it brings another increase of strength to nationalist passions.

[1] For instance, the address of the "six great industrial and agricultural associations of Germany" to Herr von Bethmann-Hollweg in May, 1914, which was not very different from that drawn up in 1815 by the Prussian metallurgists to point out to their government what annexations should be made in the interests of their industry. (See Vidal de La Blache, *La France de l'Est*, chap. xix.) Moreover, some Germans are urgent in boldly proclaiming the economic character of their nationalism. "Let us not forget," says a well-known Pan-germanist, "that the German Empire, which is generally considered abroad as a purely military State, is in its origin (Zollverein) chiefly economic." And again: "For us war is only the continuation of our commercial activity in times of peace, with other means but the same methods." (Naumann, *L'Europe Centrale*, pp. 112, 247; see the whole book.) Germany seems to be not indeed the only country to practise commercial patriotism (England has done so just as much and for a much longer time) but the only country to boast of it. . . ."

[2] And to build up a much less passionate patriotism. Think, for instance, of the agreements with foreigners accepted by patriotism based on interest (such as the Franco-German iron cartel), against which the patriotism based on pride rises up in revolt.

I shall now point out a last important perfecting of all political passions to-day, whether of race, class, party or nation. When I observe these passions in the past, I see them consisting in purely passionate impulses, natural explosions of instinct, devoid of all extension of themselves in ideas and systems—at least among the majority. The revolt of the workers in the fifteenth century against the possessing classes was apparently not accompanied by any sort of teaching about the origin of property or the nature of capital. Those who massacred the Ghettos seem to have had no views on the philosophical values of their action. And when the troops of Charles V attacked the defenders of Mezières, it does not appear that the assault was enlivened by a theory about the predestination of the Germanic race and the moral baseness of the Latin world. To-day I notice that every political passion is furnished with a whole network of strongly woven doctrines, the sole object of which is to show the supreme value of its action from every point of view, while the result is a redoubling of its strength as a passion. We must look at the system of ideology of German nationalism known as "Pangermanism" and at the similar ideology of the French Monarchists, if we wish to realize the point of perfection to which our age has carried these systems, with what tenacity each passion has built up in every direction the theories apt to satisfy it, with what precision these theories have been adapted to this satisfaction, with what opulence of research, what labor, what profound investigation they have been carried on in all directions. Our age is indeed the age of the *intellectual organization of political hatreds.* It will be one of its chief claims to notice in the moral history of humanity.

Ever since these systems have been in existence, they have consisted in establishing for each passion that it is the agent of good in the world and that its enemy is the genius of evil. But to-day these passions desire to establish this not only politically, but morally, intellectually and esthetically. Antisemitism, Pangermanism, French Monarchism, Socialism are not only political manifestations; they defend a particular form of morality, of intelligence, of sensibility, of literature, of philosophy and of artistic conceptions. Our age has introduced two novelties into the theorizing of political passions, by which they have been remarkably intensified. The first is that every one to-day claims that his movement is in line with "the development of evolution" and "the profound unrolling of history." All these passions of to-day, whether they derive from Marx, from M. Maurras or from Houston Chamberlain, have discovered a "historical law," according to which their movement is merely carrying out the spirit of history and must therefore necessarily triumph, while the opposing party is running counter to this spirit and can enjoy only a transitory triumph. That is merely the old desire to have Fate on one's side, but it is put forth in a scientific shape. And this brings us to the second novelty: To-day all political ideologies claim to be founded on science, to be the result of a "precise observation of facts." We all know what self-assurance, what rigidity, what inhumanity (comparatively new traits in the history of political passions, of which modern French monarchism is a good example) are given to these passions to-day by this claim.

To summarize: To-day political passions show a degree of universality, of coherence, of homogeneousness, of precision, of continuity, of preponderance, in relation to other passions, unknown until our times. They have become conscious of themselves to an extent never seen before. Some of them, hitherto scarcely avowed, have awakened to consciousness and have joined the old passions. Others have become more purely passionate than ever, possess men's hearts in moral regions they never before reached, and have acquired a mystic character which had disappeared for centuries. All are furnished with an apparatus of ideology whereby, in the name of science, they proclaim the supreme value of their action and its historical necessity. On the surface and in the depths, in spatial values and in inner strength, political passions have to-day reached a point of perfection never before known in history. The present age is essentially the age of politics.

II — SIGNIFICANCE OF THIS MOVEMENT — NATURE OF POLITICAL PASSIONS

WHAT IS THE SIGNIFICANCE of this movement? Of what simple and profound human tendency does it show the progress and triumph? The question comes down to inquiring what is the nature of political passions, of what more general and more essential state of mind are they the expression, what —as the schools say—is their psychological foundation?

It seems to me that these passions can be reduced to two fundamental desires: (*a*) The will of a group of men to get hold of (or to retain a hold on) some *material* advantage, such as territories, comfort, political power and all its material advantages; and (*b*) the will of a group of men to become conscious of themselves as *individuals*, insofar as they are *distinct* in relation to other men. It may also be said that these passions can be reduced to two desires, one of which seeks the satisfaction of an *interest*, the other of a *pride* or self-esteem. These two desires enter into political passions in very different proportions, according to which passion is involved. It appears that racial passion, insofar as it is not one with national passion, is chiefly based on the will of a group of men to set themselves up as distinct from others; the same thing may be said of religious passion, if we consider it in its pure state. On the other hand, class passion, at least as we see it in the working classes, apparently consists solely in the will to obtain possession of material advantages. The desire to feel himself distinct, which George Sand and the apostles of 1848 had begun to inculcate in the working man, now seems to be abandoned by him, at least in his utterances. National passion contains both factors. The patriot wants to obtain material advantages and he wants to set himself up as distinct from others. This is the secret of the evident superiority in strength of this passion (when it is really a passion) over all other passions, especially over Socialism. A passion whose sole motive is interest is too weak to contend with another which combines interest and pride. This too is one of the weaknesses of Socialism when opposed to class passion as exerted by the bourgeoisie, for the bourgeois wants both to possess material advantages and to feel himself distinct from others. I shall add to this that in my opinion the relative strengths of these two passions (one based on interest and the other on pride or self-esteem) are very unequal, and that the more powerful of the two is not that which tries to satisfy interest.

Now, when I come to ask what is signified in their turn by these fundamental desires of political passions, I find they appear to me as the two essential composites of man's will to situate himself *in real life.* To want real life is to want (*a*) To possess some material advantages, and (*b*) to be conscious of oneself as an individual. Every life which despises these two desires, every life which pursues only spiritual advantage or sincerely asserts itself in the universal, situates itself *outside the real.* Political passions, especially national passions insofar as they unite the two desires mentioned, seem to me essentially *realist* passions.

Here many persons will protest: "Yes," they will say, "the desires which make up political passions are realist desires, but the individual shifts these desires from himself to the group of which he is a part. The working man wants to obtain possession of material advantages for his class, not for his own limited person. The patriot wants to possess territories for his nation, not for his own narrow ego; he wants to be distinct from other men through his nation. Do you apply the term 'realist' to passions which imply such a transfer from the individual to the collective body?" Is it necessary to reply that when the individual transfers these desires to the body of which he is a part, he does not thereby alter their nature? And that all he does is simply to increase their dimensions immeasureably? To wish to possess material advantages *in one's nation,* to want to feel distinct from other men *in one's nation,* is still the desire to possess material advantages, still the desire to feel distinct from other men. It

35

only means that, if you are a Frenchman, you want to possess Brittany, Provence, Guyenne, Algeria, Indo-China; and you want to feel yourself distinct from other men in Jeanne d'Arc, Louis XIV, Napoleon, Racine, Voltaire, Victor Hugo, Pasteur. Add to this that at the same time you attach these desires, not to a transitory and precarious single existence, but to an "eternal" existence, and feel them in that way. Not only does national egotism not cease to be egotism because it is national, but it becomes "sacred" egotism.[1] Let me complete my definition by saying that political passions are realism of a particular quality, which is an important element of strength in them: They are *divinized* realism.[2]

If, therefore, we desire to express this perfecting of political passions which I have described, in terms

[1] "Love of country is a real love of oneself." (Saint-Evremond.)

[2] The divinizing of realism, of which patriotism specially consists, is expressed with all desirable candor in the "Addresses to the German People" (Eighth Address): Fichte attacks religion for its claim to situate the superior life outside all interest in earthly matters: "It is an abuse of religion to force it, as Christianity has so often done, to extol complete indifference to the business of the State and the nation as the true religious spirit. Men," he declares, "are determined to find heaven on earth and to impregnate their earthly labours with something durable." He then shows, with great warmth, that this desire is the essence of patriotism, and it is evident that for him earthly labors become divine by becoming durable. This, indeed, is the only means men have discovered for divinizing their institutions.

of a more profound and essential order of things, we may say that men to-day are displaying, with a hitherto unknown knowledge and consciousness, the desire to situate themselves in the *real* or practical manner of existence, in opposition to the *disinterested* or *metaphysical* manner. Moreover, it is remarkable to see how political passions to-day more and more expressly assert their derivation from this realism and from it alone. On the one hand we have a Socialism which constantly declares that it has no interest in universal man, no interest in procuring justice for him or any other "metaphysical phantom," but solely desires to obtain possession of material advantages for the benefit of its class. On the other hand we have the nationalist mind which everywhere takes a pride in being purely realistic. The French people who fought in the past to carry to other nations a doctrine they believed would bring happiness (I say the people, for its rulers never shared in that simpleminded belief) would now blush to have it even suspected that they would fight "for principles." [1] Is it not suggestive to observe that the only wars of the past which, to some extent, brought into play

[1] Is it necessary to recall that the United States did not enter the last war "in defence of principles," but with the very practical object of safeguarding their prestige, which had been lowered by the facts that the Germans had torpedoed three of their ships? Nevertheless, their desire to pose as having been purely idealistic in this affair is noteworthy.

passions that were a little disinterested—the wars of religion—are the only wars from which humanity has freed itself? [1] And that immense idealistic upheavals like the crusades (idealistic at least with humble people) should now be something which makes the modern man smile, like the spectacle of children at play? Is it not also significant that the national passions (which I have shown are the most perfectly realist of all political passions) should be those which I have been able to point out have most absorbed all other passions? [2] Let me add to this, that these passions, insofar as they are the will of a

[1] It may be said that religious passions, at least in the West, only exist as a reënforcement to national passions; in France, a man sets up as a Catholic in order to pose as being "more French"; in Germany as a Protestant in order to declare himself "more German."

[2] Here are two remarkable cases of idealistic passions which in the past successfully opposed national passion and are now submissive to it: (a) In France, the monarchic passion, which in 1792 was stronger than national feeling in many people, whereas in 1914 it was completely effaced by national feeling. (Every one will agree that attachment to a certain form of government, i.e. at bottom, the attachment to a certain metaphysical conception, is an infinitely more idealistic passion than nationalist passion; however, I do not claim that all the Emigrés were inspired by this idealism.) (b) In Germany, the religious passion, which only fifty years ago was stronger than national feeling in more than fifty per cent of Germans, and to-day is entirely subject to national feeling (in 1866 the German Catholics desired the defeat of Germany; in 1914 they ardently desired it to be victorious). The Europe of to-day, compared with the Europe of the past, seems to contain many less chances of civil wars and many more

group of men to set themselves up as distinct from others, have attained a hitherto unknown degree of consciousness.[1]   Finally, the supreme attribute we have discovered in political passions, i.e. the divinization of their realism, is now openly admitted, with a plainness never seen before.   The State, Country, Class, are now frankly God; we may even say that for many people (and some are proud of it) they alone are God.[2]   Humanity, by its present practice of political passions, thereby declares that it has become more realist, more exclusively and more religiously realist than it has ever been.

chances of national wars; nothing could show better how much Europe has lost in idealism.   (See Note D at the end of this book for additional matter on the attitude of the modern Catholics towards Catholicism when it is in opposition to their nationalism.)

[1] For example, in words like the following, uttered at Venice on the 11th December, 1926, by the Italian Minister of Education and Fine Arts: "Artists must prepare themselves for the new imperialist function which must be carried out by our art.   Above everything, we must categorically impose a principle of *Italianita*.   Whoever copies a foreigner is guilty of *lèse-nation* (an insult to the nation) like a spy who admits an enemy by a secret doorway."   These words have to be approved by every adept of *"integral* nationalism."   Moreover, we hear much the same thing in France from certain adversaries of Romanticism.

[2] "Discipline from the lowest to the highest must be essential and of a religious type."   (Mussolini, 25th October, 1925.)   This is new language in the mouth of a statesman, even of the most realist kind; it may be asserted that neither Richelieu nor Bismarck would have applied the word "religious" to an activity whose object is exclusively materialistic.

III — THE "CLERKS" — THE GREAT BETRAYAL

3.

"I created him to be spiritual in his flesh; and now he has be-come carnal even in the spirit."—(Bossuet, *Élévations*, VII, 3.)

IN ALL THAT I HAVE SAID hitherto I have been con-sidering only masses, whether bourgeois or prole-tarian, kings, ministers, political leaders, all that portion of the human species which I shall call "the laymen," whose whole function consists es-sentially in the pursuit of material interests, and who, by becoming more and more solely and sys-tematically realist, have in fact only done what might be expected of them.

Side by side with this humanity whom the poet has described in a phrase—"O curvae in terram animae et celestium inanes"—there existed until the last half century another, essentially distinct humanity, which to a certain extent acted as a check upon the former. I mean that class of men whom I shall designate *"the clerks,"* by which term I mean all those whose activity essentially is *not* the pursuit of practical aims, all those who seek their joy in the practice of an art or a science or metaphysical speculation, in short in the possession of non-material advantages, and hence in a certain manner say: "My kingdom is not of this world." Indeed, throughout history, for more than two thousand years until modern times, I see an uninterrupted series of philosophers, men of religion, men of literature, artists, men of learning (one might say almost all during this period), whose influence, whose life, were in direct opposition to the realism of the multitudes. To come down specifically to the political passions—the "clerks" were in opposition to them in two ways. They were either entirely indifferent to these passions, and, like Leonardo da Vinci, Malebranche, Goethe, set an example of attachment to the purely disinterested activity of the mind and created a belief in the supreme value of this form of existence; or, gazing as moralists upon the conflict of human egotisms, like Erasmus, Kant, Renan, they preached, in the name of humanity or justice, the adoption of an abstract principle superior to and directly opposed to these passions. Although these "clerks" founded the modern State to the extent that it dominates individual egotisms, their activity undoubtedly was chiefly theoretical, and they were unable to prevent the laymen from filling all history with the noise of their hatreds and their slaughters; *but the "clerks" did prevent the laymen from setting up their actions as a religion, they did prevent them from thinking themselves great men as they carried out these activities.* It may be said that, thanks to the "clerks," humanity did evil for two thousand years, but honored good. This contradiction was an honor to the human species, and formed the rift whereby civilization slipped into the world.

Now, at the end of the nineteenth century a fundamental change occurred: *the "clerks" began to play the game of political passions.* The men who had acted as a check on the realism of the people began to act as its stimulators. This upheaval in the moral behavior of humanity operated in several ways.

First: The "clerks" have adopted political passions.

First of all the "clerks" have adopted political passions. No one will deny that throughout Europe to-day the immense majority of men of letters and artists, a considerable number of scholars, philosophers, and "ministers" of the divine, share in the chorus of hatreds among races and political factions. Still less will it be denied that they adopt national passions. Doubtless, the names of Dante, Petrarch, d'Aubigné, certain apologists of Caboche or preachers of the Ligue will suffice to show that certain "clerks" did not wait for our era to indulge in these passions with all the strength of their souls. But, upon the whole, these "clerks" of the forum were exceptions, at least among the great ones. If, in addition to the great masters named above, I evoke the phalanx of Thomas Aquinas, Roger Bacon, Galilei, Rabelais, Montaigne, Descartes,

Racine, Pascal, Leibniz, Kepler, Huyghens, New-
ton, and even Voltaire, Buffon and Montesquieu
(to mention only a few) I think I may repeat that
until our own days the men of thought or the
honest men remained strangers to political passions,
and said with Goethe: "Let us leave politics to the
diplomats and the soldiers." Of if, like Voltaire,
they took these passions into account, they adopted
a critical attitude towards them, did not espouse
them as passions. Or if, like Rousseau, Maistre,
Chateaubriand, Lamartine, even Michelet, they
did take these passions to heart, they did so with a
generalizing of feeling, a disdain for immediate results, which in fact make the word "passions" in-
correct. To-day, if we mention Mommsen,
Treitschke, Ostwald, Brunetière, Barrès, Lemaître,
Péguy, Maurras, d'Annunzio, Kipling, we have to
admit that the "clerks" now exercise political passions with all the characteristics of passion—the
tendency to action, the thirst for immediate results,
the exclusive preoccupation with the desired end,
the scorn for argument, the excess, the hatred, the
fixed ideas. The modern "clerk" has entirely ceased
to let the layman alone descend to the market place.
The modern "clerk" is determined to have the soul
of a citizen and to make vigorous use of it; he is
proud of that soul; his literature is filled with his
contempt for the man who shuts himself up with
art or science and takes no interest in the passions

of the State.[1] He is violently on the side of Michelangelo crying shame upon Leonardo da Vinci for his indifference to the misfortunes of Florence, and against the master of the Last Supper when he replied that indeed the study of beauty occupied his whole heart. The time has long past by since Plato demanded that the philosopher should be bound in chains in order to compel him to take an interest in the State. To have as his function the pursuit of eternal things and yet to believe that he becomes greater by concerning himself with the State—that is the view of the modern "clerk." It is as natural as it is evident that this adhesion of the "clerks" to the passions of the laymen fortifies these passions in the hearts of the latter. In the first place, it abolishes the suggestive spectacle (which I mentioned above) of a race of men whose interests are set outside the practical world. And then especially, the "clerk" by adopting political passions, brings them the tremendous influence of his sensibility if he is an artist, of his persuasive power if he is a thinker, and in either case his moral prestige.[2]

Before proceeding any further, I feel I ought to make myself clear on certain points:—

(a) I have been talking of the *whole* of the men of thought anterior to our own age. When I say

[1] Notably for Renan and "speculative a-moralism." (H. Massis, *Judgments*, i.)
[2] See Note E at the end of this book for further information on this prestige, and what is new about it in history.

that the "clerks" in the past opposed the realism of the laymen and that the "clerks" of to-day are in its service, I am considering each of these groups as a whole; I am contrasting one general characteristic with another. This means that I shall not feel myself contradicted by a reader who takes pains to point out to me that so-and-so in the former group was a realist, and that so-and-so in the second is not, so long as this reader is obliged to admit that as a whole each of these groups does manifest the characteristic I have indicated. And also, when I speak of a single "clerk," I am thinking of his work in its chief characteristic, i.e. in that part of his teaching which dominates all the rest, even if the remainder sometimes contradicts this dominant teaching. This means that I do not consider that I ought to refrain from looking upon Malebranche as a master of liberal thought because a few lines of his "Morale" seem to be a justification of slavery, or upon Nietzsche as a moralist of war because the end of "Zarathustra" is a manifesto of fraternity which outdoes the Gospels. And I see the less reason for doing so, since Malebranche as a defender of slavery and Nietzsche as a humanitarian have had no influence at all, and my subject is the influence which the "clerks" have had in the world, and not what they were in themselves.

(b) Some will object to me: "How can you treat men like Barrès and Péguy as 'clerks' and blame them for lacking the true spirit of 'clerks' when they are so openly men of action, with whom political thought is obviously occupied solely with the needs of the present hour, solely spurred on by the events of the day, while the former scarcely ever gave expression to his political thought except in newspaper articles?" I reply, that this thought, which in truth is practically nothing but a form of immediate action, is given out by its authors as the fruits of the highest speculative intellectual activity, the result of the most truly philosophical meditation. Barrès and Péguy would never have consented to be looked upon as mere polemical writers, even in their polemical works.[1] These men, who indeed are not "clerks," gave themselves out to be "clerks" and were considered as such (Barrès gave himself out to be a thinker who condescended to the arena), and it is precisely as such that they enjoy a particular prestige among men of action. In this study my subject is not the "clerk" such as he is, but the "clerk" such as he is considered to be and as he acts upon the world in that capacity.

[1] In 1891 Barrès wrote to the editor of *La Plume:* "If these books have any value, it is from the logic, the continuity of thought I have put into them during five years." ("These books" included his Boulangiste campaign.) And, in the preface to his collection of articles entitled "Scènes et Documents du nationalisme," he says: "I think that if Doumic will examine it from a greater distance he will find a development, and not contradictions, in my work."

I shall make the same answer with regard to M. Maurras and the other instructors of the *Action Française,* of whom it will be said even more truly that they are men of action and that it is indefensible to cite them as "clerks." These men claim to carry out their action by virtue of a doctrine derived from a wholly objective study of history, from the exercise of the most purely scientific spirit. And they owe the special attention with which they are listened to by men of action entirely to this claim that they are *men of learning,* men who are fighting for a truth discovered in the austerity of the laboratory. They owe it to their pose as combative "clerks," but essentially *as "clerks."*

(*c*) Finally I should like to define my views on another point and to say that when the "clerk" descends to the market place I only consider that he is failing to perform his functions when he does so, like those I have mentioned, for the purpose of securing the triumph of a realist passion, whether of class, race or nation. When Gerson entered the pulpit of Notre Dame to denounce the murderers of Louis d'Orléans; when Spinoza, at the peril of his life, went and wrote the words "Ultimi barbarorum" on the gate of those who had murdered the de Witts; when Voltaire fought for the Calas family; when Zola and Duclaux came forward to take part in a celebrated lawsuit (Dreyfus affair);

all these "clerks" were carrying out their functions as "clerks" in the fullest and noblest manner. They were the officiants of abstract justice and were sullied with no passion for a worldly object.[1] Moreover, there exists a certain criterion by which we may know whether the "clerk" who takes public action does so in conformity with his true functions; and that is, that he is immediately reviled by the laymen, whose interests he thwarts (Socrates, Jesus). We may say beforehand that the "clerk" who is praised by the laymen is a traitor to his office.

But let us return to the modern "clerk's" adhesion to political passions.

It is concerning national passions that this adhesion seems to me particularly novel and big with results. Once again, of course humanity did not have to wait for the present age to see the "clerks" indulge in this passion. Without mentioning the poets, whose tender hearts have always sighed, "Nescio qua natale dulcedine solum cunctos Ducit"; and, as regards the philosophers, without going back to antiquity when all, previous to the Stoics, were ardent patriots; we may yet observe in history (since the coming of Christianity and long

---

[1] I shall be told of "clerks" who, apparently without degradation, have at some time or other taken the part of a race or a nation, even of their own race or nation. That is because they believed that the cause of that race or nation coincided at that time with the cause of abstract justice.

before our own days) writers, men of learning, artists, moralists, even ministers of the "Universal" Church, who more or less explicitly displayed a special attachment for the group to which they belonged. But this affection among these men was based on reason; it showed itself capable of judging its object, of denouncing its errors when they believed such errors had been committed. Need I recall how Fénelon and Massillon denounced certain wars of Louis XIV? How Voltaire condemned the destruction of the Palatinate? How Renan denounced the violences of Napoleon? Buckle, the intolerance of England towards the French Revolution? And, in our own times, Nietzsche, the brutalities of Germany towards France?[1] It was reserved for our own time to see men of thought, or men giving themselves out as such, professing openly that they would not submit their patriotism to any check on the part of their judgment, proclaiming (like Barrès) that "even if the country is wrong, we must think it in the right," denouncing as "traitors to the nation" those of their compatriots who retain their liberty of mind, or at least of speech, in regard to their country. In France we have not forgotten how, during the last

[1] Similar occurrences may be observed among the ancients. For instance, Cicero denounced his fellow-citizens for having destroyed Corinth merely to avenge an insult to their ambassador (De off., I, xi).

war, so many "thinkers" attacked Renan for the liberty of his judgments on the history of his country.[1] Nor have we forgotten how, a little before that, a whole set of young men (who claimed to share in the life of the spirit) bristled up against one of their masters (Jacob) who tried to teach them a patriotism which did not exclude all right of criticism. After the violation of Belgium and other excesses of the Germans, in October, 1914, a German teacher said: "There is nothing for which we need make excuses."[2] Now, if their own countries had been in a similar position, the same thing would have been said by most of the spiritual leaders of that time; by Barrès in France, by d'Annunzio in Italy, by Kipling in England, if we may judge by his conduct during the attack of his nation upon the Boers, and by William James in the United States, if we recall his attitude when his com-

[1] Already in 1911, when a writer quoted this sentence: "It is impossible to accept the situation that humanity should be bound for indefinite centuries by the marriages, battles, treaties of the narrow-minded, ignorant, egotistic creatures who during the Middle Ages were at the head of affairs in this world," he felt it necessary to add: "Fortunately these lines were written by Renan; one could not write them to-day without being called an unpatriotic Frenchman." (G. Guy-Grand, *La Philosophie Nationaliste*, p. 165.) Without being called so *by the men of thought*—that is the curious part of it.

[2] Quoted by Mgr. Chapon in his admirable study, "La France et l'Allemagne devant la doctrine chrétienne." (*Correspondant*, of 15th August, 1915.)

patriots seized the island of Cuba.[1] I am quite
ready to agree that this sort of blind patriotism
makes powerful nations, and that the patriotism of
Fénelon or of Renan is not the sort which secures
empires. It remains to determine whether the
function of "clerks" is to secure empires.

This adhesion of the "clerks" to national passion
is particularly remarkable among those whom I
shall call "preëminently clerks"; I mean the
Churchmen. In all European countries during the
past fifty years, the immense majority of these
men have not only given their adhesion to the national feeling [2] and therefore have ceased to provide
the world with the spectacle of hearts solely occupied with God—but they seem to have adopted
this feeling with the same passion as that I have
pointed out as existing among men of letters, and
they too appear to be ready to support their own
countries in the most flagrant injustices. During
the last war this could be most clearly seen in the
German clergy, from whom no one could drag the
shadow of a protest against the excesses committed
by their nation, and whose silence does not appear
to have been caused solely by prudence.[3] In con-

[1] See his *Letters*, ii, p. 31.
[2] Consider how willingly they now accept military service.
See Note F at the end of this book.
[3] Here are the reasons given by a German Catholic for this
attitude among those of his religion: "(a) Their incomplete
knowledge of the facts and opinions in the belligerent and

trast to this attitude I refer the reader to that of the Spanish theologians of the sixteenth century, to men like Bartholomew de las Casas and Vittoria, earnestly denouncing the cruelties committed by their compatriots in the conquest of America. I do not claim that similar behavior was then the rule among Churchmen, but I should like to ask whether there is a single country to-day where they would do likewise, or where they would even wish to be permitted to do so? [1]

I shall point out another characteristic of patriotism in the modern "clerk": xenophobia. The hatred of man for "the man from outside" (the *horsain*), his rejection of and scorn for everything

neutral countries; (*b*) *Their patriotism, which could not be allowed to separate itself from the union binding together the German people;* (*c*) The fear of a second Kulturkampf, which would be doubly dangerous if the German Catholics had even appeared to agree with the campaign carried on in France against German methods of waging war." The second reason will be noted, i.e. the desire to be at unity with the nation, whatever the moral aspect of its cause. Here, at least, is one reason which Bossuet did not allege when he screened the violences of Louis XIV.

Let me recall that when, in 1914, the Chancellor Bethmann-Hollweg in the Reichstag hinted at a sort of apology for the violation of Belgian neutrality, he was sharply reproved by the Christian minister von Harnack "for having tried to excuse what did not need excusing." (See A. Loisy, *Guerre et Religion*, p. 14.)

[1] The clergy of the allied nations are eager to throw in the faces of the German clergy their union with injustice in 1914. They abuse their own good fortune in belonging to nations whose cause happened to be just. When Italy, in 1923, at the

which is not "from his own home," all these impulses, so constant among peoples and apparently necessary to their existence, have been adopted in our days by the so-called men of thought, and adopted with a seriousness of application, *an absence of simple-mindedness,* which go far towards making this adoption worthy of notice. We know how systematically the mass of German teachers in the past fifty years have announced the decline of every civilization but that of their own race, and how in France the admirers of Nietzsche or Wagner, even of Kant or Goethe, were treated by Frenchmen who claimed to share in the life of the spirit.[1] You may estimate how curiously new this form of patriotism is among the men of thought in France by thinking of Lamartine, Victor Hugo, Michelet, Proudhon, Renan, to name only patriotic "clerks" in the age immediately preceding that we are considering. Is it necessary to say once again how much the "clerks" have stimulated the passion of the laymen by adopting this xenophobia?

time of the Corfu incident, adopted towards Greece an attitude as unjust as that of Austria towards Serbia in 1914, I am not aware that the Italian clergy expressed indignation. Nor do I remember that in 1900, when a European army intervened in Chinese affairs (the Boxer affair) and excesses were committed by the soldiers, any strong protests were uttered by the clergies of the respective nations.

[1] A particularly remarkable attitude was that of the philosopher Boutroux. You will find an admirable denunciation of it from the pen of Charles Andler, *Les Origines du Pangermanisme,* p. viii.

I shall be told that during the past fifty years, and especially during the twenty years before the war, the attitude of foreigners to France was such that the most violent national partiality was forced upon all Frenchmen who wished to safeguard the nation, and that the only true patriots were those who consented to this fanaticism. I say nothing to the contrary; I only say that the "clerks" who indulged in this fanaticism betrayed their duty, which is precisely to set up a corporation whose sole cult is that of justice and of truth, in opposition to the peoples and the injustice to which they are condemned by their religions of this earth. It is true indeed that these new "clerks" declare that they do not know what is meant by justice, truth, and other "metaphysical fogs," that for them the true is determined by the useful, the just by circumstances. All these things were taught by Callicles, but with this difference; he revolted all the important thinkers of his time.

It must be admitted that the German "clerks" led the way in this adhesion of the modern "clerk" to patriotic fanaticism. The French "clerks" were, and long remained, animated with the most perfect spirit of justice towards foreign cultures (think of the cosmopolitanism of the Romantics!), when already Lessing, Schlegel, Fichte, Goerres were organizing in their hearts a violent adoration for "everything German," and a scorn for everything not German. The nationalist "clerk" is essentially a German invention. This, moreover, is a theme which will frequently recur in this book, i.e. that most of the moral and political attitudes adopted by the "clerks" of Europe in the past fifty years are of German origin, and that in the world of spiritual things the victory of Germany is now complete.

It may be said that Germany, by creating for herself the nationalist "clerk" and thereby acquiring the additional strength we know she has acquired, made this species of "clerk" necessary to all other countries. It is undeniable that from the moment when Germany had a Mommsen, France especially was bound to have a Barrès, under penalty of finding herself in a position of great inferiority in nationalist fanaticism, and of seeing her existence seriously menaced. Every Frenchman attached to the continuance of his nation must rejoice that in the last half century France has possessed a fanatically nationalist literature. Yet one would like this Frenchman to rise for a moment superior to his interest, and, faithful in this to the honor of his race, to think it sad that the course of events in the world should force him to rejoice in such a thing.

More generally, it may be admitted that a realist attitude has been imposed on the modern "clerks," chiefly the French "clerks," by exterior and interior political conditions which have arisen in their nations. However serious this may be, it would be much less serious if we found that the "clerks" deplored it while they submitted to it, if they felt how much their own value is diminished by it, how greatly civilization is menaced by it, to what an extent the universe is rendered ugly by it. But this is exactly what we do not see. On the contrary, we see them joyfully carrying out this realism; we see them believing that they are rendered greater by their nationalist fury, that it is a service to civilization, an embellishment to humanity. Then one feels that one is confronted by something different from a function thwarted by the events of the moment, and faced with a cataclysm of moral notions in those who educate the world.

I should like to point out two other characteristics in the patriotism of the modern "clerks" which seem new to me, the second of which has not failed to stimulate this passion greatly among the peoples.

The first can best be brought out by contrast with the lines written by an author of the fifteenth century, lines which are the more remarkable since he who wrote them proved by his deeds how deep was his love for his native country. "All cities," says Guicciardini, "all States, all Kingdoms, are mortal; everything comes to an end, either by accident or by the course of nature. That is why a citizen who witnesses the end of his country cannot feel so distressed at her misfortune with so much reason as he would lament his own ruin. His country has met the fate which in every way she was bound to meet; the misfortune is wholly for him whose unhappy lot has caused him to be born in a time when such a disaster had to occur." One wonders whether there is a single modern thinker, attached to his country as the author of that passage was to his, who would dare to form, still less to express, a judgment of her so extraordinarily free in its melancholy. And here we come upon one of the great impieties of the moderns: The refusal to believe that above their nations there exists a development of a superior kind, by which they will be swept away like all other things. The ancients, so completely the adorers of their States, nevertheless placed them beneath Fate. The ancient City was under divine protection, but in no wise believed that she herself was divine and necessarily eternal. All the literature of the ancients shows us that, in their opinion, the duration of their institutions was a precarious thing, solely due to the favor of the Gods, who at any time might withdraw that favor.[1] We have Thucydides contem-

[1] This may be seen especially in the chorus of the Seven against Thebes: "Gods of our City, let it not be destroyed with our houses and our hearths. . . . O ye who have dwelt therein so long, will ye betray this land?" Six centuries later this may be seen in the "Aeneid," where the preservation of

plating the image of a world in which Athens should have ceased to exist; we have Polybius showing us the conqueror of Carthage meditating over the burning town: "And Rome too shall meet her fatal hour." We have Virgil praising the peasant of the fields for whom "res romanae et peritura regna" are of no value.

It was reserved for the moderns to make of their City a tower which defies the heavens, and to do it with the aid of their "clerks."

The second characteristic of the patriotism of the modern "clerks" is a desire to relate the form of their own minds to a form of the *national* mind, which they naturally brandish against other national forms of mind. We all know how, during the last fifty years, so many men of learning on both banks of the Rhine have asserted their views in the name of *French* science, of *German* science. We know how acridly so many of our writers in the same period have vibrated with *French* sensibility, *French* intelligence, *French* philosophy. Some declare that they are the incarnation of Aryan thought, Aryan painting, Aryan music, to which others reply by discovering that a certain master had a Jewish grandmother, and so venerate Semitic genius in him. Here it is not a question of inquir-

the Trojan City across the seas is plainly due solely to the protection of Juno, and in no wise to any inward notion of Trojan blood giving it an assurance of eternal duration.

61

ing whether the form of mind of a scholar or an artist is the signature of his nationality or his race and to what extent, but of noting the desire of the modern "clerks" that it should be so, and noting how new a thing this is. Racine and La Bruyère never dreamed of setting up their works before themselves and before the world as manifestation of the French mind, nor did Goethe and Winckle-mann relate theirs to the genius of Germany.[1] Here, chiefly among the artists, is a very remark-able fact. It is very remarkable to see men whose activity consists, one might say professionally, in the assertion of individuality, men who became so violently conscious of this truth a century ago with the Romantic movement, now (as it were) ab-dicating this sort of consciousness and trying to feel themselves as the expression of some general

---

[1] Although the Germans appear to have been the inventors of the passion I am denouncing, Lessing and Schlegel seem to have been the first to brandish their poets as the expression of the national soul, from a feeling of exasperation with the uni-versalism of French literature. The men of the French Pléïade (who will certainly be brought up against me) wished to give their sensibility a national mode of expression, a na-tional language; they never claimed to give a national char-acter to that sensibility, to oppose it to other national sensi-bilities. The systematic nationalization of the mind is un-doubtedly an invention of modern times. As regards the men of learning, this nationalizing has undoubtedly been favored by the disappearance of Latin as the scientific language; and no one will ever be able to say to what an extent this disap-pearance was an element of arrest in civilization.

existence, a manifestation of a collective mind. It is true that this abdication of the individual in favor of "a great impersonal and eternal Whole" satisfies another sort of Romanticism. It is true that this impulse of the artist may also be explained by the desire (which Barrès does not conceal) to increase the enjoyment of himself by himself, since the consciousness of the individual ego is doubled in profundity by consciousness of the national ego, while at the same time the artist finds new lyrical themes in this second consciousness. It may also be admitted that the artist is not blind to his own interest in calling himself the expression of the genius of his nation, thereby inviting the whole race to applaud itself in the work he put before it.[1] Whatever their motives may have been, the great minds or the minds reputed such, by relating the whole of their value so noisily to their nation, have labored in a direction contrary to that expected of them; they have flattered the vanity of nations, they have fed full the arrogance with

[1] In Nietzsche's opinion, this was the case with Wagner, who, when he gave himself out to his compatriots as the Messiah of German art, saw that there was "a good vacant place to take," while the whole of his artistic formation as well as his profound philosophy, was essentially universalist. (See *Ecce Homo*, p. 58. "What I have never forgiven Wagner is his condescending to Germany.") One wonders whether the same might not be said of a certain apostle of "Lorrain genius" or of "Provençal genius."

which each nation flings its superiority in the face of its neighbors.[1]

I cannot better bring out all the novelty of this attitude of the "clerk" than by quoting the remark of Renan, which would be signed by all men of thought from Socrates onwards: "Man belongs neither to his language nor to his race; he belongs only to himself, for he is a free being, that is, a moral being." To this Barrès replies, amid the applause of his compeers: "To be moral is *not to wish to be free from one's race.*" Here, obviously, is an exaltation of the gregarious spirit which the nations had heard little of before from the priests of the spirit.

The modern "clerks" do better still. They declare that their thought cannot be good, that it cannot bear good fruit, unless they remain on their native soil, unless they are not "uprooted" ("*déracinés*"). They congratulate A on working in *his* Bearn, B in *his* Berry, C in *his* Brittany. And they not only proclaim this law for the poets, but for critics, moralists, philosophers, the servants of purely intellectual activity. To declare the mind

---

[1] The nationalization of the mind sometimes has results whose savor is not sufficiently enjoyed. In 1904, during the centenary celebrations of Petrarch, the nations of Goethe and Shakespeare were not invited, because they are not Latins; but the Roumanians were invited. We do not know whether Uruguay was invited.

good to the extent of its refusal to liberate itself from the earth is something which will make the modern "clerks" certain of a conspicuous place in the annals of the spiritual life. Obviously, the feelings of this class of men have changed since Plutarch taught: "Man is not a plant created to be immobile and to have his roots fixed in the soil where he was born," and since Antisthenes replied to his colleagues who boasted that they were native to the soil, that "they shared this honour with the slugs and grasshoppers."

Need I say that I am only denouncing this desire of the "clerk" to feel himself determined by his race and to remain fixed to his native soil to the extent that it becomes in him a political attitude, a nationalist provocation. The best way for me to define this is by quoting this hymn of a modern "clerk" to "his soil and his dead," a hymn completely void of political passion:

"And the old oak under which I am sitting speaks in its turn, and says to me:

" 'Read, read in my shadow those Gothic songs whose refrains I heard in the past mingle with the rustling of my leaves. The souls of your ancestors are in these songs that are older than I am. Learn to know those humble ancestors, share their past joys and sorrows. Thus, O transitory creature, shalt thou live long ages in a few years. Be pious,

venerate the soil of your country. Never take up
a handful in your hand without remembering that
it is sacred. Love all those far-off relatives whose
dust mingled with earth has fed me for centuries,
whose minds have passed into you, their Benjamin,
the child of better days. Reproach not your ancestors with their ignorance, nor with the feeble-
ness of their thought, nor even with the illusions
of fear which sometimes rendered them cruel. As
well reproach yourself for having been a child.
Remember that they laboured, that they suffered,
that they hoped for you, and that you owe everything to them!' " [1]

[1] Anatole France, *La Vie Littéraire,* tome ii, p. 274. The
nationalist desires in French writers which I have been pointing out have had other than political results; no one will ever
be able to say how many among them in the past fifty years
have falsified their talents, mistaken their true gifts in their
endeavors to "feel in the French manner." A good example
is the *Voyage de Sparte,* where so many pages show what a
beautiful piece of work it might have been if the author had
not *forced* himself to feel his Lorrain soul under a Greek sky.
Here we come upon one of the most curious characteristics in
the writers of this age; the rejection of freedom of mind *for
themselves,* the thirst for "a discipline" (the whole fortune of
MM. Maurras and Maritain comes from this), a thirst which
in most of them is the result of a fundamental intellectual
nihilism. (On this nihilism in Barrès, see Curtius, "Barrès and
the intellectual foundations of French nationalism," extracts
in *Union pour la Verite,* May, 1925; in Maurras, see Guy-
Grand, op. cit., p. 19; and L. Dimier, *Vingt Ans d'Action
Française,* p. 330: "I have never seen a more unhappy soul
than his.") But the psychology of contemporary writers in
itself and apart from its political action is not my subject here.

*Second: They bring their political passions into
their activities as "clerks."*

The "clerks" have not been content simply to
adopt political passions, if by this one means that
they have made a place for these passions side by
side with the activities they are bound to carry on
as "clerks." They have introduced these passions
into those activities. They permit, they desire
them to be mingled with their work as artists, as
men of learning, as philosophers, to color the essence of their work and to mark all its productions.
And indeed never were there so many political
works among those which ought to be the mirror
of the disinterested intelligence.

You may refuse to be surprised by this in the
case of poetry. We must not ask the poets to separate their works from their passions. The latter
are the substance of the former, and the only question to ask is whether they write poems to express
their passions or whether they hunt for passions in
order to write poems. In either case one does not
see why they should exclude national passion or the
spirit of party from their vibrant material. Our
political poets, who are not numerous however,
have only followed the example of Virgil, Claudian,
Lucan, Dante, d'Aubigné, Ronsard, and Hugo.
Yet we cannot deny that political passion, as it is

expressed by Claudel or d'Annunzio, a conscious and organized passion *lacking all simplicity,* coldly scornful of its adversary, a passion which in the second of these poets displays itself as so precisely political, so cunningly adapted to the profound cupidity of his compatriots and the exact point of weakness in the foreigner—we cannot deny, I say, that this political passion is something different from the eloquent generalities of the "Tragiques of the Année Terrible." A work like *La Nave,* with its national plan as exact and practical as that of a Bismarck wherein the lyric gift is used to extol this practical character, seems to me something new in the history of poetry, even of political poetry. The result of this new departure on the minds of laymen may be judged by the present state of mind of the Italian people.[1] But in our day the most remarkable example of the poets' applying their art to the service of political passions is that literary form which may be called "lyrical philosophy," the most brilliant symbol of

[1] I think it novel that a poet should give rise to a demonstration so essentially practical as the address of the Naval League of Venice to d'Annunzio after the publication of *La Nave.* "On the day when your genius radiates with new splendour over the ancient ruler of 'our sea,' over Venice, to-day disarmed against Pola, the Naval League of Venice thanks you with emotion, hoping that the third Italy may at last arm the prow and set sail towards the world." (*Translator's Note.*—I have rendered the French version as quoted; its meaning or lack of meaning is no doubt inherent in the genius of the original, which I have not before me.)

which is the work of Barrès. It begins by taking as its centers of vibration certain truly philosophical states of mind, such as pantheism, a loftily skeptical intellectualism) and then entirely devotes itself to serving racial passion and national feeling. Here the action of the lyric spirit is doubled by the prestige of the spirit of abstract thought (Barrès admirably caught the appearance of that spirit— he stole the tool, a philosopher has said of him), and in France as elsewhere the "clerks" have thereby stimulated political passions among the laymen, at least in that very important section of them who read and believe they think. Moreover, in regard to poets and especially the poet I have just named, it is difficult to know whether the lyrical impulse lends its aid to a genuine and preëxisting political passion, or whether on the contrary this passion puts itself at the service of a lyrical impulse which is seeking inspiration. Alius judex erit.

But there are other "clerks" who introduce political passion into their works with a remarkable consciousness of what they are doing, in whom this derogation seems more worthy of notice than in the poets. I mean the novelists and dramatists, i.e. "clerks" whose function is to portray in as objective a manner as possible the emotions of the human soul and their conflicts—a function which, as Shakespeare, Molière, and Balzac have proved, may be carried out with all the purity I have here assigned to it. One may show how this function has been more than ever perverted by its subjection to political ends by the example of many contemporary novelists, not because they scatter "tendencious" reflections throughout their narratives (Balzac constantly does so), but because instead of making their heroes feel and act in conformity with a true observation of human nature, they make them do so as the passion of the authors requires. Shall I cite those novels where the traditionalist, whatever his errors, always finally displays a noble soul, whereas the character without religion inevitably, and in spite of all his efforts, is capable of none but vile actions? [1] Or the other novels where the man of the people possesses every virtue and vileness is the exclusive portion of the bourgeois? [2] Or the novels where the author displays his compatriots in contact with foreigners and, more or less frankly, gives all moral superior-

[1] Compare with Balzac, who, though a Conservative, never hesitates to show his Conservatives and particularly his Catholics in an unfavorable light, if he thinks that the true light. See the examples quoted by E. Seillière (*Balzac et la morale romantique,* pp. 27 onwards, and 84 onwards), who sharply reproaches Balzac.

[2] *"Resurrection," "Jean-Christophe"* (derived in this respect from the procedure of George Sand). On the other hand, I seem to find a great deal of justice done the bourgeois in *Les Misérables,* which is nevertheless a most "tendencious" novel.

ity to his own people? [1] There is a two-fold evil in this proceeding; not only does it considerably inflame political passion in the breast of the reader, but it deprives him of one of the most eminently civilizing effects of all works of art, i.e. that self-examination to which every spectator is impelled by a representation of human beings which he feels to be true and solely preoccupied with truth. [2] From the point of view of the artist and of the value of his activity alone, this partiality indicates a great degradation. The value of the artist, the thing which makes him the world's high ornament, is that he *plays* human passions instead of living them, and that he discovers in this "play" emotion the same source of desires, joys and sufferings as ordinary men find in the pursuit of real things. Now, if this accomplished type of exuberant activity places itself at the service of the nation or of a class, if this fine flower of disinterestedness becomes utilitarian, then I say with the poet of the "Vierge aux Rochers" when the author of *Siegfried* exhales his last sigh: "The world has lost its import."

I have pointed out that certain "clerks" have put their activities as "clerks" at the service of political

[1] For instance, pre-war French novels showing the French in Alsace-Lorraine. We may be quite certain that since 1918 the Germans have written novels which are the exact counterpart to these.
[2] See Note G at the end of this book.

passions. These are the poets, the novelists, the dramatists, the artists, i.e. they are men who may be permitted to give passion, even willful passion, a predominant place in their works. But there are other "clerks" in whom this derogation from the disinterested activity of the mind is far more shocking, "clerks" whose influence on the laymen is much more profound by reason of the prestige attached to their functions. I mean the historians. Here, as with the poets, the phenomenon is a new one on account of the point of perfection it has reached. Assuredly, humanity did not await our age to see History putting itself at the service of the spirit of party or of national passion. But I think I may assert that it has never seen this done with the same methodical spirit, the same intensity of consciousness which may be observed in German historians of the past half century and in the French Monarchists of the past twenty years. The case of the latter is the more remarkable since they belong to a nation which has acquired eternal honor in the history of human intelligence by explicitly condemning pragmatic history and formulating, as it were, the charter of disinterested history, through the works of Beaufort, Fréret, Voltaire, Thierry, Renan, Fustel de Coulanges.[1] Yet the

[1] See, for instance, Fustel de Coulanges's study *De la manière d'écrire l'histoire en France et en Allemagne*. It will be observed that this author's denunciation of the German historians exactly applies to certain French historians of recent years, with this difference: That the German alters history to exalt

true novelty here is the admission of this spirit of partiality, the expressed intention to employ it as a legitimate method. "A true German historian," declares a German master, "should especially tell those facts which conduce to the grandeur of Germany." The same scholar praises Mommsen (who himself boasted of it) for having written a Roman history "which becomes a history of Germany with Roman names." Another (Treitschke) prided himself on his lack of "that anemic objectivity which is contrary to the historical sense." Another (Guisebrecht) teaches that "Science must not soar beyond the frontiers, but be national, be German." Our Monarchists do not lag behind. Recently one of them, the author of a *History of France,* which tried to show that the French Kings since Clovis were occupied in trying to prevent the war of 1914, defended the historian who presents the past from the point of view of the passions of his own time.[1] By his determination in bringing this partiality to historical narrative the modern "clerk" most seriously derogates from his true function, if I am right in saying that his function is to restrain

his nation and the Frenchman to exalt a political system. In general it may be said that the "tendencious" philosophies of the Germans lead to national war, and those of the French to civil war. Is it necessary to repeat, after so many others, how much this proves the moral superiority of the latter?

[1] *Revue Universelle,* 15th April, 1924. Here is that very curious desire of the moderns to yield to subjectivism, whereas their elders made every effort to combat it.

the passions of the laymen. Not only does he inflame the laymen's passions more cunningly than ever, not only does he deprive them of the suggestive spectacle of a man solely occupied by the thirst for truth, but he prevents the laymen from hearing speech different from that of the market place, speech (Renan's is perhaps the finest example) which, coming from the heights, shows that the most opposite passions are equally justified, equally necessary to the earthly State, and thereby incites every reader who has any capacity for getting outside himself to relax the severity of his passions, at least for a moment.

Let me say, however, that indeed men like Treitschke and his French equivalents are not historians; they are men of politics who make use of history to support a cause whose triumph they desire. Hence, it is natural that the master of their method should not be Lenain de Tillemont but Louis XIV, who threatened to withdraw Mezeray's pension if the historian persisted in pointing out the abuses of the old monarchy; or Napoleon, who ordered the chief of police to take measures for the history of France to be written in a manner favorable to his own throne. Nevertheless, the really cunning ones assume the mask of disinterestedness.[1]

I believe that many of those whom I am here

---

[1] See Note H at the end of this book.

accusing of betraying their spiritual ministry, that disinterested activity which should be theirs by the mere fact of their being historians, psychologists, moralists, would reply to me as follows, if such a confession did not destroy their influence: "We are not in the least the servants of spiritual things; we are the servants of material things, of a political party, of a nation. Only, instead of serving it with the sword, we serve it with the pen. We are *the spiritual militia of the material.*"

Among those who ought to show the world an example of disinterested intellectual activity and who nevertheless turn their function to practical ends, I shall also mention the critics. Every one knows that innumerable critics to-day consider that a book is only good insofar as it serves the party which is dear to them, or as it manifests "the genius of the nation," or as it illustrates a political doctrine in harmony with their own political system, or for other reasons of the like purity. The modern "clerks," I said before, insist that the just shall be determined by the useful. They also want the useful to determine the beautiful, which is not one of their least originalities in history. Nevertheless, here again those who adopt such a form of criticism are not truly critics, but men of politics, who make criticism serve their practical designs. Here is a perfecting of political passion, the whole honor of which must be given to the moderns.

Neither Pius XIV nor Napoleon apparently thought of using literary criticism in support of the social system in which they believed.[1] This new departure has brought forth its fruits. For instance, if you assert with the French Monarchists that the democratic ideal is inevitably bound up with bad literature, you are dealing that ideal a real blow in a country like France, which has a real devotion to literature, at least among those who will consent to believe that Victor Hugo and Lamartine were mere scribblers.[2]

But the most remarkable thing about the modern "clerk" in his desire to bring political passion into his work, is that he has done so in philosophy, more precisely, in metaphysics. It may be said that until the nineteenth century metaphysics remained the inviolate citadel of disinterested speculation. Among all forms of spiritual labor metaphysics best deserved the admirable tribute which a mathematician rendered the theory of numbers above all branches of mathematics, when he said: "This is the really pure branch of our science, by which I mean that it is unsullied by any contact with practical application." In fact thinkers free from

[1] Yet the Jesuits thought of doing so to combat the Jansenists. (See Racine, Port-Royal, pt. i.)
[2] On the matter of the lack of literary sensibility which accompanies this political criticism among its adepts, see a paragraph of L. Dimier, Vingt Ans d'Action Française, p. 334.

any sort of earthly preference, like Plotinus, Thomas Aquinas, Descartes, Kant, and even thinkers strongly imbued with the superiority of their class or nation (like Plato and Aristotle), never thought of directing their transcendental speculations towards a demonstration of this superiority or the necessity of this adoption by the whole world. It has been said that the morality of the Greeks was national, but their metaphysics were universal. The Church itself, so often favorable to class or national interests in its morality, thinks only of God and Man in its metaphysics. It was reserved for our own age to see metaphysicians of the greatest eminence turning their speculations to the exaltation of their own countries and to the depreciation of other countries, fortifying the will to power of their compatriots with all the power of abstractive genius. Fichte and Hegel made the triumph of the German world the supreme and necessary end of the development of Being, and history has showed whether the action of these "clerks" had an effect on the hearts of their laymen. Let me hasten to add that this spectacle of patriotic metaphysics is provided by Germany alone. In France, even in this age of nationalist "clerks," we have not yet seen any philosopher (at least one who is taken seriously) build up a metaphysical system to the glory of France. Neither

Auguste Comte nor Renouvier nor Bergson ever thought of making a French hegemony the necessary result of the world's development. Need I add what a degradation this has been for metaphysics, as it has been for art? It will be the eternal shame of the German philosophers to have transformed the patrician virgin who honored the Gods into a harpy engaged in shrieking the glory of her children.

Third: The "clerks" have played the game of political passions by their doctrines.

But where the "clerks" have most violently broken with their tradition and resolutely played the game of the laymen in their eagerness to place themselves in the real, is by their doctrines, by the scale of values they have set up for the world. Those whose preaching for twenty centuries had been to humiliate the realist passions in favor of something transcendental, have set themselves (with a science and a consciousness which will stupefy history) to the task of making these passions, and the impulses which ensure them, the highest of virtues, while they cannot show too much scorn for the existence which in any respect raises itself beyond the material. I shall now describe the principal aspects of this phenomenon.

*A. The "clerks" praise attachment to the partic-
ular and denounce the feeling of the universal.*

In the first place, the "clerks" have set out to
exalt the will of men to feel conscious of themselves
as distinct from others, and to proclaim as contemptible every tendency to establish oneself in a
universal. With the exception of certain authors
like Tolstoi and Anatole France, whose teaching
moreover is now looked on with contempt by most
of their colleagues, all the influential moralists of
Europe during the past fifty years, Bourget, Barrès,
Maurras, Péguy, d'Annunzio, Kipling, the immense majority of German thinkers, have praised
the efforts of men to feel conscious of themselves
in their nation and race, to the extent that this
distinguishes them from others and opposes them
to others, and have made them ashamed of every
aspiration to feel conscious of themselves as men
in the general sense and in the sense of rising above
ethnical aims. Those whose activity since the time
of the Stoics had been devoted to preaching the
extinction of national egotism in the interest of an
abstract and eternal entity, set out to denounce
every feeling of this kind and to proclaim the
lofty morality of that egotism. In our age the descendants of Erasmus, Montaigne, Voltaire, have
denounced humanitarianism as a moral degenera-

tion, nay, as an intellectual degeneration, in that it implies "a total absence of practical common sense"; for practical common sense has become the measure of intellectual values with these strange "clerks."

I should like to draw a distinction between humanitarianism as I mean it here—a sensitiveness to the abstract quality of what is human, to Montaigne's "whole form of human condition"—and the feeling which is usually called humanitarianism, by which is meant the love for human beings existing in the concrete. The former impulse (which would more accurately be called humanism) is the attachment to a concept. It is a pure passion of the intelligence, implying no terrestrial love. It is quite easy to conceive of a person plunging into the concept of what is human without having the least desire even to see a man. This is the form assumed by love of humanity in the great patricians of the mind like Erasmus, Malebranche, Spinoza, Goethe, who all were men, it appears, not very anxious to throw themselves into the arms of their neighbors. The second humanitarianism is a state of the heart and therefore the portion of plebeian souls. It occurs among moralists in periods when lofty intellectual discipline disappears among them and gives way to sentimental exaltation, I mean in the eighteenth century (chiefly with Diderot) and above all in the nineteenth century, with Michelet, Quinet, Proudhon, Romain Rolland, Georges Duhamel. This sentimental form of humanitarianism and forgetfulness of its conceptual form explain the unpopularity of this doctrine with so many distinguished minds, who discover two equally repulsive commonplaces in the arsenal of political ideology. One of them is "the patriotic bore" and the other "the universal embrace." [1]

The humanitarianism which holds in honor the abstract quality of what is human, is the only one which allows us to love *all* men. Obviously, as soon as we look at men in the concrete, we inevitably find that this quality is distributed in different quantities, and we have to say with Renan: "In reality one is *more or less* a man, *more or less* the son of God . . . I see no reason why a Papuan should be immortal." Modern equalitarians, by failing to understand that there can be no equality

[1] The distinction between these two humanitarianisms is well expressed by Goethe when he relates (Dichtung und Wahrheit) the indifference of himself and his friends to the events of 1789. "In our little circle, we took no notice of news and newspapers; our object was to know Man; as for men, we left them to do as they chose." Need I recall that the "humanities," as instituted by the Jesuits in the seventeenth century, the "studia humanitatis," are "the study of what is most essentially human," in no sense altruistic exercises. See further Note I at the end of this book for a curious quotation from one of the ancients.

except in the abstract and that inequality is the
essence of the concrete, have merely displayed the
extraordinary vulgarity of their minds as well as
their amazing political clumsiness.[1]

Humanism, as I have defined it, has nothing to
do with internationalism. Internationalism is a
protest against national egotism, not on behalf of
a spiritual passion, but on behalf of another egotism, another earthly passion. It is the impulse of
a certain category of men—laborers, bankers, in-
dustrialists—who unite across frontiers in the name
of private and practical interests, and who only
oppose the national spirit because it thwarts them
in satisfying those interests.[2]

In comparison with such impulses, national passion appears an idealistic and disinterested impulse.
In short, humanism is also something entirely different from cosmopolitanism, which is the simple
desire to enjoy the advantages of all nations and all
their cultures, and is generally exempt from all

[1] This the Church has understood so well, and the corollary
to this truth: That love between men can only be created by
developing in them the sensibility for abstract man, and by
combating in them the interest for concrete man; by turning
them towards metaphysical meditation and away from the
study of history (see Malebranche). This is exactly the contrary direction to that of the modern "clerks," but, once again,
these "clerks" have not the slightest desire to create love
among men.

[2] Thus they adopt the national spirit if it seems to serve
their interests; for instance, the party of "nationalist-
socialists."

moral dogmatism.[1] But let us come back to this movement of the "clerks" exhorting the peoples to feel conscious of themselves in what makes them distinct from others.

What will especially amaze history in this movement of the "clerks" is the perfection with which they have carried it out. They have exhorted the peoples to feel conscious of themselves in what makes them *the most distinct* from others, in their poets rather than in their scientists, in their legends rather than in their philosophies, since poetry (as they perfectly well perceived) is infinitely more national, more separating than the products of pure intelligence.[2] They have exhorted the peoples to

[1] Certain nationalists, desirous of honoring cosmopolitanism, whose full value their intelligence perceives, and yet not wishing to sacrifice nationalism, declare that cosmopolitanism represents "enlightened nationalism." M. Paul Bourget, who gives this definition (*Paris-Times*, June, 1924), quotes Goethe and Stendhal as examples, "the former of whom remained so profoundly German while striving to understand the whole movement of French thought, and the latter remained so profoundly French while he devoted himself to understanding Italy." One wonders how these two masters showed the least, even enlightened, "nationalism" by remaining profoundly German and profoundly French. Obviously M. Bourget confuses national and nationalist.

[2] Almost all works of national propaganda among the small nations of Eastern Europe are anthologies of poetry. Very few are works of thought. See the words uttered by E. Boutroux in August, 1915, to the Committee of the Entente Cordiale, against the peoples who attach too much importance to the intelligence, which "of itself tends to be one and common to all beings capable of knowledge."

83

honor their poets' characteristics insofar as they are peculiar to them and are not universal. Recently a young Italian writer praised his language because it is only used in Italy, and poured scorn on French because it is employed universally.[1] They have exhorted the peoples to feel conscious of themselves in *everything* which makes them distinct from others, not only in their language, art, and literature, but in their dress, houses, furniture, and food. During the past half century it has been a common experience to see serious writers (to go no further than France) exhorting their compatriots to remain faithful to French fashions, French hair-dressing, French dining rooms, French cooking, French cars. They have exhorted the peoples to feel themselves distinct even in their vices. The German historians, says Fustel de Coulanges, urge their nation to be intoxicated with its personality, even to its barbarity. The French moralist does not lag behind and desires his compatriots to accept their "national determinism" in its "indivisible totality," with its injustices as well as its wisdom, with its fanaticism as well as its enlightenment, its pettiness as well as its grandeur. Another (Maurras), declares: "Good or bad, our tastes are ours and it is always permissible to take ourselves as the sole judges and models of our lives." Once again, the remarkable thing here is not that

[1] *Les Nouvelles Littéraires*, 25th September, 1926.

84

such things should be said, but that they should be said by the "clerks," by a class of men whose purpose hitherto has been to urge their fellow-citizens to feel conscious of themselves in what is common to all men, that they should be said in France by the descendants of Montaigne, Pascal, Voltaire, and Renan.

This glorifying of national particularism, so unexpected among all "clerks" is especially so among those whom I described as "preëminently clerks"— the Churchmen. Those who for centuries have exhorted men, at least theoretically, to deaden the feeling of their differences in order to take cognizance of each other in the divine essence which brings all men together, have now come to praise them, according to where the sermon is given, for their "fidelity to the French soul," for "the immutability of their German consciousness," for the "fervour of their Italian hearts." [1] The sight is indeed surprising and remarkable! What would be thought by him who, by the mouth of his apostle, declared: "There is neither Greek nor Jew nor barbarian, but Christ is in all things," if to-day he

[1] Here is a specimen of the acrobatics which these teachers are compelled to perform in order to conciliate Christian doctrine with the preaching of national particularisms: "We wish to set the ideal of universalism in positive relation to the contemporary reality of the national form, which is that of all life, even the Christian life." (Pastor Witte, quoted by A. Loisy, *Guerre et Religion*, p. 18.) Here are minds for whom the squaring of the circle is obviously mere child's play.

entered one of his churches and saw offered to the veneration of his faithful, a national heroine with a sword on her thigh and a flag in her hand? [1]

This glorification of national particularisms, at least with the precision observable to-day, is undoubtedly something new in the history of the Church. It is not necessary to go back as far as Saint Augustine, who preached the extinction of all patriotisms in the embrace of "the City of God"; nor even to Bossuet, who shows us the indignation of Jesus at observing "that because we are separated by a few rivers or mountains, we seem to have forgotten that we are all of one nature." So recently as 1849 a lofty assembly of prelates asserted that "this movement of nationalities is a relic of paganism, differences of language are a consequence of sin and the fall of man." Certainly this declaration was an interested one, since it was provoked by the Most Catholic Francis Joseph to check the separatist tendencies among the peoples of his Empire; but I dare to assert that the Church would no longer make such a declaration, even for motives of interest. I shall be told that even if the Church wished to do so, she could only do it under penalty of delivering up her ministers to a terrible unpopularity among their respective peoples. As if the

[1] Is it not suggestive to note that the Church in the last twenty years has replaced the commandment "Homicide shalt thou not be, in fact or by assent" with "Homicide shalt thou not be, without right, nor voluntarily"?

"clerk's" function were not to tell the laymen truths which are displeasing to them, and to pay the price at the expense of his own peace!

I do not ask so much. Is there a single prelate in any pulpit of Europe who would now dare to pronounce: "The Christian is both a cosmopolitan and a patriot. These two qualities are not incompatible. The world indeed is one common fatherland, or, to speak in more Christian terms, one common exile." (Pastoral letter "On the pretended philosophy of modern infidels," by Le Franc de Pompignon, Bishop of Puy, 1763. The "infidels" here are those who refuse the Church the right to be cosmopolitan.)

Some "clerks" do better, and assert that by extolling national particularisms they are in complete harmony with the fundamental spirit of the Church, especially with the teaching of the great Doctors of the Middle Ages. (This is the thesis which opposes Catholicism to Christianity.) Need I recall the fact that the most national of these Doctors limited themselves to considering national particularisms as an inevitable condition of an earthly and inferior world, which must be respected like everything else which is the will of God? Or that they never exhorted men to intensify this feeling in their hearts, still less did they ever think of putting this intensification before them as an exercise in moral self-perfection?

When the Church in past times did approve of something in patriotism, it was fraternity among fellow-citizens, like love of man for other men, but not his opposition to other men. She approved of patriotism as an extension of human love, and not as a limitation of it.[1]

But the most remarkable thing in all this is that recently—precisely since the time when Benedict XV was reproached during the last war for not having denounced the arrogance of German nationalism—there has arisen a school in the bosom of the Church which tries to prove that by acting in this way the Holy Father had simply obeyed the teaching of his Divine Master, who is supposed to have preached explicitly the love of a man for his own nation. Could anything better symbolize the

[1] For example in this passage of Bossuet: "Since we are obliged to love all men and since in truth no man is a foreigner to a Christian, there is all the more reason for loving our fellow citizens. All the love a man feels for himself, for his family, and for his friends is united in the love he feels for his country. . . ." (*Politique tirée de l'Ecriture Sainte*, I, vi. Notice the phrase "All the love a man feels for himself. . . ." It wholly justifies Saint Evremond's phrase: "Love of country is really love of oneself.") It appears that the Church would prefer to go on presenting patriotism under this one aspect of love (see the inquiry of "les Lettres" on the Church and Nationalism, 1922-3), which would allow her to exalt this passion (as its popularity requires) without violating the principles of Christianity. Unfortunately for the Church, positive men come along and remind her that patriotism is something more than love, and includes "hatred for the foreigner." (Maurras, *Dilemme de Marc Sangnier*.) Who will deliver us from the truth-tellers?

determination of the modern "clerks" to place their credit and their activities at the service of lay passions than these Churchmen making Jesus an apostle of nationalism?

These strange Christians express themselves thus:

"Jesus does not look beyond the frontiers of his own country with the idea of bestowing his benefactions upon other nations. He declares to the Canaanitish woman, whose daughter he heals against his own wish, that 'his mission is only to the lost sheep of the house of Israel' (Matt. xv, 24). He sent his first disciples among the Israelites. And notice how he insists that they shall not go elsewhere. 'Go not on the paths of the Gentiles, and enter not the cities of the Samaritans, but go first to the lost sheep of the house of Israel.' (Matt. x, 6.) Later on, it will be time enough to announce the good news to foreigners, but first of all we must bring it to our own people. This is what he means by the words, so full of patriotic meaning and love: 'the house of Israel.' A group of human beings possessing the same blood, the same language, the same religion, the same tradition, form 'a house.' These particularities are so many dividing walls." [1]

They also say:

"The most striking thing about Jesus when he consents to pay tribute to Caesar and refuses the

[1] A. Lugan, *La grande loi sociale de l'amour des hommes,* liv. ii, chap. iii.

89

crown which the people offer him in the desert, is not so much his prudence and his disinterestedness, as his patriotism. . . . One of the most important characteristics of Jesus's teaching is its absolutely national character. . . ." [1]

If the reader desires, he will himself go and find out the solidity of the proofs on which these teachers base their thesis (one of these proofs is that Jesus was strongly attached to the institutions of his nation, which he showed by accepting circumcision eight days after he was born). The point I wish to insist on is the eagerness of these Christians to make their Master a supporter of national egotism, at least at one period of his life.

These views on the attitude of the Church towards nationalism seem to me to remain unmodified by the recent declarations of the Holy See concerning a certain type of French nationalism, for these declarations only condemn an openly anti-Christian nationalism (hence a very exceptional form of nationalism) and do not utter a word of blame for the desire of the peoples to set themselves up as distinct from others and to reject universalism. Moreover, this is how a universalist is answered by a publication which is to some extent the official organ of Pontifical views:

"Yes, all men are sons of one Father; but they were divided in the beginning and have never been

---

[1] Père Ollivier, *Les Amitiés de Jesus*, p. 142.

brought together again. The family was broken up and never joined up again. On the contrary. Certainly, I am glad to recognize the fraternity of all living beings; but are all the dead our fathers? Have they all loved us? Have they all suffered and laboured for us? Some lived on the other side of the globe, and, so to speak, in another world. Some laboured against us, or, if they supported our ancestors, it was in the hope of safeguarding or enriching their own bequest to others, not to us. Where is the debt? If the home is open to all comers, it is no longer a home but an inn." [1]

It appears that we must look among those who have left the Church, to find Christian ministers who proclaim the true teaching of their Master, and who declare with no beating about the bush: "The Gospel of Jesus does not imply any country, but obliterates the fatherland." [2]

The modern "clerk" denounces the feeling of universalism, not only for the profit of the nation, but for that of a class. Our age has beheld moralists who have declared to the bourgeois world (or to the working classes) that, far from trying to check

---

[1] *Dictionnaire apologétique de la foi catholique* (1919), in the article headed "Patrie." The reader will note the extraordinary practical spirit of this article, and the desire to love only those who have done something for us.

[2] Loisy's *Guerre et Religion*, p. 60. Nevertheless, a certain number of practicing clergy speak in the same way; see Guillot de Givry, *Le Christ et la Patrie*, towards the end.

the feeling of their differences from others and to feel conscious of their common human nature, they should on the contrary try to feel conscious of this difference in all its profundity and irreducibleness, and that this effort is fine and noble, whereas every desire for union is here a sign of baseness and cowardice, and also of weakness of mind. This, as every one knows, is the thesis of the *Reflections on Violence,* which has been praised by a whole galaxy of apostles of the modern soul. There is certainly something more novel in this attitude of the "clerks" to class differences than in their attitude towards national differences. To discover the results of this teaching and the additional hatred (hitherto unknown) which it has given to either class in doing violence to its adversary, you have only to look at Italian Fascism for the bourgeois class, and at Russian Bolshevism for the working class.[1]

Here again we see realism trying to shelter under cover of the Church. We see certain Catholic teachers striving to prove that, by encouraging the bourgeois class, *in the name of morality,* to feel

[1] It is current knowledge that Italian Fascism and Russian Bolshevism both derive from the author of *Reflections on Violence.* He did, indeed, preach class egotism to some extent in a universal manner, but without any explicit preference for the interest of one class rather than that of another. In his preaching of egotism there is a kind of impartiality which does not lack grandeur, a quality not inherited by his disciples.

92

conscious of themselves as distinct from the opposing class, to plunge religiously into consciousness of the characteristics which are proper to their own class, and especially (Johannet) to *intensify their feeling of property*, these teachers are merely acting in conformity with the teaching of the Church.[1]

It is easy to point out the equivocation upon which this claim is based. The Church does indeed admit class distinctions. She exhorts the faithful to recognize and even to respect them, as something imposed by God upon a fallen world. She also exhorts the privileged to accept their situation, to carry out the activities it implies, and to perform "the duties of their state of life." She even tells them that by performing these duties they are pleasing God and "making an act of prayer." But the Church never exhorted them to glorify in themselves the feeling of this distinction, still less did she ever do so in the name of morality. On the con-

[1] And even the teaching of Jesus Christ. R. Johannet says (op. cit., p. 153), "I have tried to show what a vast amount of Christianity is contained in the bourgeois type, when it is pure. To condemn the bourgeois, because he is a bourgeois, in the name of Christ, seems to me a somewhat daring paradox." But this author does not quote a single text of the Gospels. He only quotes a few interpreters of Saint Thomas Aquinas, whom he praises for their "extra-realist sense of affairs," and who apparently for him incarnate the thinking of Jesus Christ. This work is one of the most perfect examples of the modern "clerk's" desire to idealize the practical spirit. (On the subject of Christian doctrine in the matter of property, see Father Thomassin, *Traité de l'aumône*.)

trary, she exhorted them in the name of morality to extinguish (beneath this privileged life) all belief in a particularity of essence in their persons, and told them to feel conscious of themselves in that humanity which is common to all men beneath the inequality of ranks and states of life.[1] Jesus Christ, the Church states explicitly and constantly, *only accepts the man who is reconciled*, i.e. the man who has obliterated from his heart every feeling of difference between himself and other men. (See Bossuet's *Sermon on Reconciliation*.) It seems unnecessary to insist further on the unimpeachable character of this Christian teaching—I am speaking of teaching, not of practice. But one cannot meditate too much on the eagerness of so many modern Church teachers to try to find some means of sanctifying bourgeois egotism through the words of the Gospels.[2]

[1] It might be said that in Christian theology the bourgeois state is a *function*, and not a rank.

[2] The essential position of the Church on this point (I say essential; for, by close search, one can find texts supporting the opposite thesis, but once more the curious thing is the fact that this search should be made) seems to me defined in these lines: "Malebranche inclines, like Bossuet, to look upon social inequalities and injustices as the results of sin, which must be endured as such, and to which exterior conduct must conform. . . . We must not even attempt to remedy these injustices except by charity, for we should simply disturb the peace of the world, probably without any result. Only, *we should not in our own souls attach any sort of importance to these circumstances and conditions, for the true life is not there*" (H. Joly, *Malebranche*, p. 262).

Let me point out another and remarkable form of this extolling of particularism by the "clerks": the extolling of particular systems of morality and the scorn for universal morality. During the past half century a whole school, not only of men of action but of serious philosophers, has taught that a people should form a conception of its rights and duties from a study of its particular genius, its history, its geographical position, the particular circumstances in which it happens to be, and not from the commands of a so-called conscience of man in all times and places. Moreover, this same school teaches that a class should construct a scale of good and evil, determined by an inquiry into its particular needs, its particular aims, the particular conditions surrounding it, and should cease to encumber itself with such sensibilities as "justice in itself," "humanity in itself" and other "rags and tatters" of general morality. To-day with Barrès, Maurras, Sorel, even Durckheim [1] we are witnessing the complete bankruptcy among the "clerks" of that form of soul which, from Plato to Kant, looked for the notion of good in the heart of eternal and disinterested man. The example of Germany in 1914 shows the results of this teaching which exhorts a group of men to set themselves up as the

[1] On the relation between Durckheim's theses and those of the French traditionalists, see D. Parodi, *La Philosophie contemporaine en France*, p. 148.

95

sole judges of the morality of their actions, shows what deification of their appetites it leads to, what codification of their violence, what tranquillity in carrying out their plans. One day perhaps we shall see the same thing throughout Europe exemplified by the bourgeois class, unless the doctrines of that class are turned against itself and we see it exemplified by the working classes.[1]

I dare to say that the indignation of certain French moralists at the action of Germany in 1914 surprises me, when I reflect that some sixteen years earlier, during the famous "affair" which I have already mentioned, these moralists preached to their compatriots exactly the same doctrines, urging them to reject the concept of absolute justice, and to desire only a form of justice "adapted to France," to its particular genius, its particular history, its particular, eternal, and present needs.[2] For the honor of these thinkers—I mean for the honor of

---

[1] "Germany is the sole judge of her methods." (Major von Disfurth, November, 1914.) The philosophy of national moralities seems essentially German. Is it not very remarkable to see Hegel and Zeller desiring at all costs to prove that Plato in his *Republic* defined a state of good which was only valid for the Greeks, and not for all peoples? (See P. Janet, *Histoire des idées politiques,* tome 1, p. 140.)

[2] Barrès wrote in 1898: "The professors are still arguing about justice and truth, when every self-respecting man knows that he must limit himself to inquiring if there is justice in the relations between two given men, at a given time, under specified circumstances." That is exactly what the Germany of 1914 said in answer to those who brought accusations

their consistency—one likes to think that their indignation in 1914 was not the result of any moral
conviction, but only of the desire to place the
enemy of their nation in the wrong with a naïve
universe.

This last-named activity of the "clerks" seems to
me one of those which best display their determination and skill in serving the passions of the laymen.
If a man exhorts his compatriots to recognize only
a personal morality and to reject all universal
morality, he is showing himself a master of the art
of encouraging them to want to be distinct from
all other men, i.e. of the art of perfecting national
passion in them, at least in one of its aspects. The
desire to take none but oneself as a judge of one's
actions and to scorn every opinion of other people
is undoubtedly a source of strength to a nation, as
every exertion of pride is a source of strength to an
institution, whose fundamental principle—whatever may be said to the contrary—is the assertion of
an ego against a non-ego. What ruined Germany
in the last war was not its "irritating arrogance," as
is asserted by certain visionaries who have made up
their minds that malevolence of soul must be an
element of weakness in practical life, but the fact
that its material strength was not equal to its arro-

against her. Not a single moralist in France before Barrès—
not even de Maistre or Bonald—would have asserted that
"every self-respecting man" can conceive of no justice but
one specially arranged for the circumstances.

gance. When arrogance finds an equivalent material power at its disposal, it is very far from ruining nations; witness Rome and the Prussia of Bismarck. The "clerks" who, thirty years ago, exhorted France to make herself the sole judge of her own actions and to despise eternal morality, showed that they possessed in the highest degree the perception of the national interest, insofar as that interest is wholly realist and has nothing to do with disinterested passion. It remains to be seen, once more, whether the function of the "clerks" is to serve this sort of interests.

But the modern "clerks" have held up universal truth to the scorn of mankind, as well as universal morality. Here the "clerks" have positively shown genius in their effort to serve the passions of the laymen. It is obvious that truth is a great impediment to those who wish to set themselves up as distinct; from the very moment when they accept truth, it condemns them to be conscious of themselves in a universal. What a joy for them to learn that this universal is a mere phantom, that there exist only particular truths, "Lorrain truths, Provençal truths, Britanny truths, the harmony of which in the course of centuries constitutes what is beneficial, respectable, *true in France*" [1] (the neigh-

[1] *L'Appel au Soldat.* Compare this with the traditional French teaching, of which Barrès claims to be the heir: "Whatever your country may be, you should only believe what you

bor similarly speaks of what is *true in Germany*),
that in other words Pascal had the mind of a clown,
and that what is true on one side of the Pyrenees
may perfectly well be error on the other side! Humanity hears the same teaching about the classes
and learns that there is a bourgeois truth and a
working-class truth; better still, that the function-
ing of our minds should be different according to
whether we are working men or bourgeois. The
source of your troubles (Sorel teaches the working
classes) is that you do not think in the mental way
suited to your class. His disciple, Johannet, says
the same thing to the capitalist class. Perhaps we
shall soon see the results of this truly supreme art
of the "clerks" in exasperating the feeling of their
differences among the classes.

The cult for the particular and the scorn for the
universal is a reversal of values quite generally characteristic of the teaching of the modern "clerks,"
who proclaim them in a far higher sphere of
thought than politics. The metaphysics adopted in
the last twenty years by almost all those who think
or pretend to think, set up as the supreme state of
human consciousness that state—"duration"—

would be disposed to believe if you were in another country."
(*Logique de Port-Royal*, iii, xx.) It must not be thought that
dogma of national truths aims only at moral truth. Recently
certain French thinkers waxed indignant that the doctrines of
Einstein were accepted by their compatriots without more
resistance.

where we succeed in taking cognizance of ourselves in what is most individual, most distinct from everything not ourselves, and in freeing ourselves from those forms of thought (concept, reason, habits of speech) through which we can only become conscious of ourselves in what is common to us and others. These metaphysics put forward as a superior form of cognizance of the world that which grasps each thing by what is unique in it, distinct from every other, and is full of scorn for the mind which seeks to discover general states of being. Our age has seen a fact hitherto unknown, at least from my point of view; and this in metaphysics preaching adoration for the contingent, and scorn for the eternal.[1] Nothing could show better how profound is the modern "clerk's" desire to exalt the real, the practical side of existence, and to

[1] The adoration of the contingent *for its own sake;* otherwise, and as a step towards the eternal, the knowledge of "strange things" is highly recommended by Leibniz, and even by Spinoza. Renouvier, so hostile to a certain kind of universalism, never bestows philosophical value on a knowledge of what is "unique and inexpressible" in the object. (See G. Seailles, "Le Pluralisme de Renouvier," *Revue de Metaphysique et de Morale,* 1925.) He would never have signed this charter of modern metaphysics: "That the philosophers since Socrates should have contended as to which should most scorn the knowledge of the particular and should most adore knowledge of the general, is something which passes understanding. For, after all, must not the most honourable knowledge be the knowledge of the most valuable realities! And is there a valuable reality which is not concrete and individual?" (William James.)

degrade the ideal, the truly metaphysical side. In the history of philosophy this veneration for the individual comes from the German thinkers (Schlegel, Nietzsche, Lotze), while the metaphysical cult of the universal (added to a certain contempt for the experimental) is preëminently a legacy of Greece to the human mind. So here again, and moreover in its profoundest part, the teaching of the modern "clerks" shows the triumph of Germanic values and the bankruptcy of Hellenism.

I should like to point out another form, not the least remarkable, which this preaching of particularism assumes among the "clerks." I mean their exhortations to consider everything only as it exists *in time*, that is as it constitutes a succession of particular states, a "becoming," a "history," and never as it presents a state of permanence beyond time under this succession of distinct cases. I mean especially their assertion that this view of things in their historical aspect is the only serious and philosophical view, and that the need to look at them in their eternal aspect is a form of the child's taste for ghosts, and should be merely smiled at. Need I point out that this conception inspires the whole of modern thought? It exists among a whole group of literary critics, who, on their own showing, inquire far less whether a work is beautiful than whether it expresses "the present" aspirations of "the contemporary soul." [1] It may be seen in a whole school of moralist-historians who admire a doctrine, not because it is just or good, but because it embodies the morality *of its time,* the scientific spirit *of its time.* (This is the principal reason why Sorel admires Bergsonism and why Nietzsche admires the philosophy of Nicolas de Cuse.) It may be seen especially in all our metaphysicians. Whether they put forward *Entwickelung* or *Duration* or *Creative Evolution* or *Pluralism* or *Integral Experience* or the *Concrete Universal,* they all teach that the absolute is developed *in time,* in the circumstantial, and proclaim the decadence of that form of mind which, from Plato to Kant, hallows existence as conceived beyond change. [2] If, with Pythagoras, we assume that the Cosmos is the place of regulated and uniform existence, and the

[1] An important literary review recently reproached a critic (M. Pierre Lasserre) for his supposed inaptitude to understand "contemporary literature."

[2] Curiously enough, these metaphysics of the historic may also be found among the poets. We all know Claudel's cult of "the present minute" (because it differs from all other minutes in that it is not the extremity of the same quantity of the past); Rimbaud before this said: "One must be absolutely modern." Moreover, for certain Christians dogma is only valid *relative to a time.* There again particularism seems to have been started by the Germans: "No exposition of morality can be the same for all periods of the Christian Church; each possesses full and complete value for a certain period only." (Scheiermacher.) On the Germanism in this desire to see everything in its "becoming," see Parodi, *le Problème moral et la Pensée contemporaine,* p. 255.

Ouranos the place of the becoming and the moving, we may say that all modern metaphysics place the Ouranos at the top of their scale of values and hold the Cosmos in very slight esteem. Is it not remarkable to see the "clerks," even in the lofty function of metaphysicians, teaching the laymen that the real alone is worthy of consideration, and that the supersensible is only worthy of derisive laughter? [1]

(B) The "clerks" praise attachment to the practical, and denounce love of the spiritual

But the "clerks" with their doctrines have inflamed the realism of the laymen in other ways besides praising the particular and denouncing the universal. At the very top of the scale of moral values they place the possession of concrete advantages, of material power and the means by

[1] These views on the modern cult of the particular do not seem to me to be invalidated by the arrival of a recent school (Neo-Thomism) which opposes the cult of Being to that of Becoming. According to the leaders of this school, it is clear that, despite certain universalist declarations, human Being really belongs only to them and their group, although in this case the group is wider than the nation. One of them would quite willingly say with a Christian of the second century: "We are men; the rest are pigs and dogs." Nor do I think I need take into account those particularisms which claim that by working for themselves they are working for the universal, seeing that for them their own group represents the universal. "I am Roman, I am human" (Maurras). "I am German, I am human (Fichte)" and so on. . . . However, these claims show the prestige of the universal in despite of doctrines.

which they are procured; and they hold up to scorn the pursuit of truly spiritual advantages, of non-practical or disinterested values.

This they have done, first of all, as regards the State. For twenty centuries the "clerks" preached to the world that the State should be just; now they proclaim that the State should be strong and should care nothing about being just. (Remember the attitude of the chief French teachers during the Dreyfus affair.) Convinced that the strength of the State depends upon authority, they defend autocratic systems, arbitrary government, the reason of State, the religions which teach blind submission to authority, and they cannot sufficiently denounce all institutions based on liberty and discussion.[1] This denunciation of liberalism, notably by the vast majority of contemporary men of letters, will be one of the things in this age most astonishing to History, especially on the part of the French. With their eyes fixed on the powerful State, they have praised the State disciplined in the Prussian manner, where every one has his post, and under orders from above, labors for the greatness of the nation, without there being any place left for particular wills.[2] Owing to their cult of the powerful State (and also for other reasons I shall

[1] See Note J at the end of this book.
[2] On the cult of the "Prussian model" even among the English "clerks," see Elie Halévy, *Histoire du Peuple anglais*, Epilogue, livre ii, ch. i.

mention later), they want the military element to preponderate in the State, they want it to have a right to privileges and they want the civil element to agree to this right. (See *L'Appel au Soldat*, and the declarations of numerous writers during the Dreyfus affair.) It is certainly something new to see men of thought preaching the abasement of the toga before the sword, especially in the country of Montesquieu and Renan. And then they preach that the State should be strong and contemptuous of justice, above all in its relations with other States. To this end they praise in the head of the State the will to aggrandisement, the desire for "strong frontiers," the effort to keep his neighbors under his domination. And they glorify those means which to them seem likely to attain these ends, i.e. sudden aggression, trickery, bad faith, contempt for treaties. This apology for Machiavellianism has inspired all the German historians for the past fifty years, and in France it is professed by very influential teachers, who exhort France to venerate her Kings because they are supposed to have been models of the purely practical spirit, exempt from all respect for any silly justice in their relations with their neighbors.

The novelty of this attitude among the "clerks" can best be displayed by quoting the famous answer of Socrates to the realist in the *Georgias*:

"In the persons of Themistocles, Cimon and

Pericles, you praise men who made their fellow citizens good cheer, by serving them with everything they desired without caring to teach them what is good and right in food. They have enlarged the State, cry the Athenians, but they do not see that this enlargement is nothing but a swelling, a tumour filled with corruption. This is all that has been achieved by these former politicians by filling the city with ports, arsenals, walls, tributes, and the like follies, and by not adding Temperance and Justice."

Up to our own times, in theory at least (but it is with theories I am dealing here) the supremacy of the spiritual proclaimed in those words has been adopted by all those who, explicitly or otherwise, have proposed a scale of values to the world, whether through the Church, or the Renaissance, or the eighteenth century. One can guess the derisive laughter of a Barrès or any Italian moralist (to speak only of the Latin races) at this disdain of power for the benefit of justice, and their severity for the manner in which this son of Athens judges those who made his city materially powerful. For Socrates, in this respect the perfect model of the "clerk" who is faithful to his essential function, ports, arsenals, walls are "follies," and the serious things are justice and temperance. Those who to-day should perform the duties of a Socrates consider that it is justice which is a folly—"a cloud"—

and the serious things are the arsenals, the walls. To-day the "clerk" has made himself Minister of War. Moreover, one of the most revered modern moralists definitely approves of the judges who condemned Socrates, as good guardians of worldly interests.[1] And that is something which has not been seen among the educators of the human soul since the evening when Crito closed his master's eyelids.

I say that the modern "clerks" have *preached* that the State should be strong and care nothing about being just; and in fact the "clerks" do give this assertion the characteristic of preaching, of moral teaching. I cannot insist too often that in this lies their great originality. When Machiavelli advises the Prince to carry out the Machiavellian scheme of action, he invests those actions with no sort of morality or beauty. For him morality remains what it is for every one else, and does not cease to remain so because he observes (not without melancholy) that it is incompatible with politics. "The Prince," says Machiavelli, "must have an understanding always ready to do good, but he must be able to enter into evil when he is forced to do so"; thereby showing that for him evil, even if it aids politics, still remains evil. The modern realists are the *moralists* of realism. For them, the act which makes the State strong is invested with

[1] Sorel, *Le procès de Socrate.*

107

a moral character by the fact that it does so, and this whatever the act may be. The evil which serves politics ceases to be evil and becomes good. This position is evident in Hegel, in the Pangermanists and in Barrès; it is no less evident among realists like M. Maurras and his disciples, in spite of their insistence in declaring that they profess no morality. Perhaps these teachers do not profess any morality, at least expressly, in what concerns private life, but they very clearly profess a morality in the political order of things, if by morality is meant everything which puts forward a scale of good and evil. For them as for Hegel, the practical in politics *is the moral,* and if what the rest of the world calls moral is in opposition to the practical, then *it is the immoral.* Such precisely is the perfectly moralist meaning of the famous campaign of "false patriotism." It seems as if we might say that for M. Maurras the practical is the divine, and that his "atheism" consists less in denying God than in shifting Him to man and his political work. I think I can describe the work of this writer accurately by saying that it is the *divinizing of politics.*[1] This displacement of morality is undoubtedly

[1] This has been perfectly obvious to all those guardians of the spiritual who have condemned it, whatever their motives may have been. More precisely, Maurras's work makes the passion of man to found the State (or to strengthen it) an object of religious adoration; it is really the worldly made transcendental. This displacing of the transcendental is the

the most important achievement of the modern "clerks," and the most deserving of the historian's attention. It is a great turning-point in the history of man when those who speak in the name of pondered thought come and tell him that his political egotisms are divine, and that everything which labors to relax them is degrading. The results of this teaching were shown by the example of Germany a decade ago.[1]

The extent to which the modern "clerks" have

secret of the great influence exerted by Maurras on his contemporaries. These persons, especially in irreligious France, were plainly eager for such a doctrine, if one may judge by the outburst of gratitude with which they greeted it, and which seems to say: "At last we are delivered from God; at last we are allowed to adore ourselves in our will to be great, not in our will to be good; we are shown the ideal in the real, on earth and not in heaven." In this sense, Maurras's work is the same as Nietzsche's ("be faithful to the earth"), with this difference, that the German thinker deifies man in his anarchic passions, and the Frenchman in his organizing passions. It is also the same as the work of Bergson and James, inasmuch as it says like them: the real is the only ideal. This *secularizing of the divine* may be compared with the work of Luther.

[1] Machiavellian morality is plainly proclaimed in the following lines, where every open-minded person will recognize, except for the tone, the teaching of *all* the present teachers of realism, whatever their nationality: "In his relations with other States, the Prince should know neither law nor right, except the right of the strongest. These relations place in his hands, under his responsibility, the divine rights of the Destiny and government of the world, and raise him above the precepts of individual morality into a higher moral order, whose content is enshrined in the words: Salus popu li suprema lex esto." (Fichte, quoted by Andler, op. cit., p. 33.) The advance on Machiavelli is obvious.

made innovations may be judged by the fact that up till our own times men had only received two sorts of teaching in what concerns the relations between politics and morality. One was Plato's, and it said: "Morality decides politics"; the other was Machiavelli's, and it said: "Politics have nothing to do with morality." To-day they receive a third. M. Maurras teaches: "Politics decide morality." [1] However, the real departure is not that this doctrine should be put before them, but that they should accept it. Callicles asserted that force is the only morality; but the thinking world despised him. Let me also mention that Machiavelli was covered with insults by most of the moralists of his time, at least in France.

The modern world also hearkens to other moralists of realism, who are not lacking in influence as such; I mean the statesmen. Here I shall point to the same sort of change as above. Formerly, leaders of States practiced realism, but did not honor it; Louis XI, Charles the Fifth of Spain, Richelieu, Louis XIV, did not claim that their actions were moral. They saw morality where the Gospel had showed it to them, and they did not attempt to

---

[1] The teaching of this writer may be put in this form: "All that is good from the point of view of politics is good; *and I know no other criterion of good.*" This enables him to say that he makes no pronouncement in matters of private morality.

displace it because they did not apply it.[1] With them morality was violated, but moral notions remain intact; *and that is why, in spite of all their violence, they did not disturb civilization.* Signor Mussolini proclaims the morality of his politics of force and the immorality of everything which opposes it. Like the writer, the man of government, who formerly was merely a realist, is now the *apostle* of realism; and the majesty of his function —if not of his person—gives weight to his apostleship.

The modern governor, owing to the fact that he addresses crowds, is compelled to be a moralist, and to present his acts as bound up with a system of morality, a metaphysics, a mysticism. Richelieu, who need account only to his King, is able to talk only of the practical, and leaves visions of the eternal to others. Mussolini, Bethmann-Hollweg,

---

[1] In Richelieu's *Testament politique* and the *Mémoires de Louis XIV pour l'Instruction du Dauphin*, the catalogue of good and ill might be signed by Saint Vincent de Paul. We read in them: "Kings should take care in making treaties, but once the treaties are made, *they must observe them religiously.* I know that many politicians teach the contrary; but, without taking into consideration all that the Christian Faith provides us with against these maxims, I maintain that since the loss of honour is greater than the loss of life itself, a great Prince should hazard his person and *even the interest of his State rather than break his word,* which he cannot violate without losing his reputation and consequently *the greatest strength* of a Sovereign." (*Testament Politique,* part 2, ch. vi.)

Herriot, are condemned to these heights.[1] More-over, this shows how great to-day is the number of those whom I can call "clerks," since by that word I mean all those who speak to the world in a tran-scendental manner. Consequently, I have a right to demand that they give an account of their acts *as "clerks."*

The preachers of political realism often claim to base themselves on the teaching of the Church, and call her a hypocrite when she condemns their theses. This claim has little foundation as regards the teaching of the Church before the nineteenth cen-tury, but has much more foundation if we consider the present age. I doubt whether one could now find from the pen of a modern theologian any pas-sage so brutally denunciatory of a war of aggres-sion as the following:—

"Glaringly unjust is the war of him who de-clares war only from ambition and from the desire

---

[1] Similarly with the writer—Machiavelli, who writes for his peers, can allow himself the luxury of not being a moralist; Maurras who writes for crowds cannot do so. No one writes with impunity in a democracy. Moreover, a political activity which is supported by moral activity proves that it under-stands the true conditions of its success. A master in these matters says: "There can be no profound political reform un-less religion and morality are also reformed." (Hegel.) Clearly the particular influence of the *Action Française* among all other conservative organs is due to the fact that its political movement is supported by a moral teaching, although other interests oblige it to deny this.

to extend his dominions beyond their legitimate boundaries, from the desire to possess a more commodious country in which to establish himself, from the fear of the great power of a neighbouring prince with whom he is at peace, or from the desire to despoil a rival solely because he is thought unworthy of the possessions or States he holds or of a right which legitimately belongs to him, because a ruler is inconvenienced by him and wants to get rid of this inconvenience by force of arms." [1] On the other hand, there are an immense number of works to-day which need only a little twisting to make them justify every attempt at conquest. For instance, the view that a war is just "if it can invoke the necessity of safeguarding the common good and public tranquillity, the recapture of things unjustly carried off, the repression of rebels, the defence of the innocent." [2] And the view which asserts that "war is just when it is necessary to a nation either to defend itself against invasion, or *to overthrow*

---

[1] *Dictionnaire des Cas de Conscience* (ed. 1712), article "Guerre." With such a morality the territorial formation of any European State would become impossible. This is the type of non-practical teaching, i.e. of what I mean by the true "clerk." (See Note F at the end of this book on the subject of the welcome given to this teaching by the material world.) In the opinion of Vittoria as well, the extension of empire is not a just cause.

[2] This is the thesis of Alfonso Liguori which to-day prevails in the Church's teaching over that of Vittoria.

THE TREASON OF THE INTELLECTUALS

the obstacles thwarting the exercise of its rights." [1]
At the beginning of the last century the Church
still taught that war could only be just for one of
the two belligerents.[2] It is heavy with consequences that she has now abandoned this position
and to-day asserts that war may be just on both
sides at once, "from the moment when each of the
two adversaries, without being certain of its right,
considers it as simply probable after having taken
the opinion of its counsellors." [3] Here is another
serious thing: In the past, war would only be declared just when it was against an adversary who
had committed an injury *accompanied by a moral
intention,* whereas to-day it may be declared just
if it is directed against a material injury caused

[1] Cardinal Gousset (*Théologie morale,* 1845).

[2] This is the Scholastic doctrine of war, formulated in all
its rigidity by Thomas Aquinas. According to this doctrine,
the Prince (or the people) who declares war, acts as a magis-
trate (minister Dei) under whose jurisdiction a foreign nation
falls, owing to an injustice it has committed and which it
refuses to repair. From this it follows, in particular, that the
Prince who has declared war ought solely to punish the guilty,
if he is victorious, and not to acquire any personal benefit from
his victory. This high moral doctrine is entirely abandoned by
the Church to-day. (See Vanderpol, *La Guerre devant le
Christianisme,* titre ix.)

[3] Apparently this was the view adopted by the Holy See in
1914 towards the Franco-German war, Germany benefiting by
what theology calls "invincible" ignorance, i.e. implying that
one has used all the diligence of which a man is capable in
trying to understand the explanations of an adversary. Obviously, one may feel that some goodwill was needed to think
that Germany had a right to this benefit.

without any malice,[1] for instance, an accidental violation of frontier. It is certain that to-day Napoleon and Bismarck could find in the teaching of the Church more justification than ever for their incursions.[2]

The modern "clerks" have preached this realism to the classes as well as to the nations. They say to the working class as well as to the bourgeois class: "Organize yourselves, become the stronger, seize on power or exert yourself to retain it if you already possess it; laugh at all efforts to bring more charity, more justice or any other 'rot'[3] into your

[1] Like the thesis of war being just on both sides, this is the doctrine of Molina, which in matters of law in war has entirely replaced Scholastic doctrine in ecclesiastic teaching.

[2] In the *Dictionnaire théologique* of Vacant-Mangenot (1922, article "Guerre"), I find the following passage, which I recommend to all aggressors desirous of sheltering under a high moral authority: "It is not only the right but the duty of the leader of a nation to adopt this method (i.e. war) to safeguard the general interests committed to his care. This right and duty apply not only to a strictly defensive war, but also to an offensive war rendered necessary by the actions of a neighbouring State whose ambitious intrigues constitute a real danger." In the same article will be found a theory of colonial wars identical to Kipling's when he calls them: *the white man's burden*.

[3] This expression (i.e. "la blague") is Sorel's (see Julien Benda, *Les Sentiments de Critias*, p. 258); and again (*Reflexions sur la Violence*, ch. ii): "You cannot sufficiently execrate those who teach the people that they should carry out some alleged superlatively idealistic injunction of a justice moving towards the future." Moreover, Sorel professes a similar hatred for those who preach this injunction to the bourgeoisie.

relations with the other class, you have been cheated long enough by that sort of thing." And here again they do not say: "Become so, because necessity demands it." They say, and that is the novelty of it: "Become so, because morality, esthetics demand it; to wish to be powerful is the sign of an elevated soul, to wish to be just the sign of a base soul." This is the teaching of Nietzsche,[1] of Sorel, applauded by a whole thinking (so-called) Europe; this is the enthusiasm of Europe, when it is attracted by Socialism, for the doctrines of Marx, its scorn for the doctrines of Proudhon.[2] The "clerks" have said the same thing to the parties contending within the same nation. "Make yourself the stronger," they say to one or other, according to their own passion, "and do away with everything which obstructs you; free yourself from the foolish prejudice which exhorts you to make allowances for your adversary, to establish with him a system of justice and harmony." We all know the admiration professed by a whole army of "thinkers" in all countries for the Italian government, which simply outlaws all citizens who do not approve of it. Until our own times the educators of the human soul,

[1] See Note K at the end of the book.
[2] See *Reflexions sur la Violence*, ch. vi: "The morality of Violence." We shall be told that the justice denounced by Sorel is the justice of tribunals, which according to him is a false justice, a "violence with a judicial mask." There is no indication that a justice which was a true justice would receive any more respect from him.

disciples of Aristotle, urged mankind to denounce as infamous any State which was an organized faction. The pupils of Signor Mussolini and M. Maurras learn to reverence such a State.[1]

This extolling of the "strong State" by the modern "clerks" appears also in certain teachings which, it may be asserted, would greatly have amazed their ancestors, at least the great ones:—

(a) *The affirmation of the rights of custom, history, the past* (to the extent, be it understood, that they support the systems of force) in opposition to the rights of reason. I say the affirmation of the *rights* of custom. The modern traditionalists do not simply teach, like Descartes or Malebranche, that custom is upon the whole quite a good thing, and that there is more wisdom in submitting to it than opposing it. They teach that custom has a right, *the* right, and consequently that custom should be respected not only from the point of view of interest, but of justice. The arguments in favor of the "historical right" of Germany to Alsace, the "historical right" of the French monarchy, are not purely political positions, they are moral positions. They claim to be accepted in the name of "true

---

[1] In this respect one cannot stress too much in certain political teachers a defense of intolerance, carried out with a consciousness and arrogance which hitherto had only appeared sometimes in the mandatories of a revealed religion. A specimen is quoted by G. Guy-Grand (*La Philosophie nationaliste*, p. 47). See also one of these defenses in L. Romier, *Nation et Civilisation*, p. 180.

justice," of which (they say) their adversaries have a false conception.[1] To determine what is just by the "accomplished fact" is certainly a new sort of teaching, especially among the peoples who for twenty centuries derived their conception of what is just from the companions of Socrates. Here again, the soul of Greece has given place to the soul of Prussia among the educators of mankind. The spirit which speaks here—and from all the teachers of Europe, Mediterranean as well as Germanic—is the spirit of Hegel: "The history of the world is the justice of the world." (*Weltgeschichte ist Weltgericht.*)

(*b*) The extolling of *policy founded on experience*—by which is meant that a society should be governed on principles which have proved that they can make it strong, and by "illusions" which would tend to make it just. It is in this narrowly practical sense that the cult of experimental politics is a new thing among the "clerks." For if we mean by the phrase the respect for principles which have

---

[1] Modern science has established as the measure of truth, not the deductive demands of its understanding, but the observed existence of the fact." (Paul Bourget.) The "truth" here is evidently moral truth; for scientific truth the phrase would be a tautology. Once more, here the "fact" is solely the fact which happens to suit the author's passions. When M. d'Haussonville points out to M. Bourget that democracy is a fact, and an unavoidable fact, he is told that this belief is a "prejudice" and one suddenly learns that "boats are made to row against the stream." This is exactly what revolutionaries say.

showed that they are fitted to make a society not only strong but just, the recommendation of such a policy in opposition to a purely rational policy appeared in the thinking world long before the disciples of Taine or Auguste Comte.[1] Long before our "organizing empiricists" Spinoza wanted political science to be an experimental science, and desired that the conditions under which States endure should be sought from observation at least as much as from reason. (See his attack on the Utopians, *Treatise*, 1, i.) But he believed he learned from observation that these conditions do not solely consist in States possessing good armies and obedient peoples, but in their respecting the rights of citizens and even of neighboring peoples.[2] The cult of experimental politics to-day is accompanied in those who adopt it by a posture which they evidently mean to be striking, and which in fact is so. We all know with what fatalistic visages, what scornful inflexibility, what dark

[1] See Note L at the end of this book.

[2] Another thinker to whom our empiricists are strangely ungrateful is the author of these words: "Consider the danger of one stirring up the enormous masses which form the French nation. Who could restrain the disturbance set up, or foresee all the results it might produce? Even if all the advantages of the new scheme should be indisputable, what man of good sense would dare to undertake to abolish old customs, to change old maxims, and to give a new form to a State other than that it has reached after an existence of 1,300 years? (J. J. Rousseau.)

certainty of grasping the absolute, they declare that in matters of politics "they consider only the facts." Here, especially among the French thinkers, is a new kind of Romanticism, which I shall call the *Romanticism of Positivism,* the chief representatives of which will rise up in the imagination of my readers without its being necessary for me to name them. Moreover, this cult brings out a silliness of mind which to me seems wholly an acquisition of the nineteenth century,[1] i.e. the belief that the teachings to be drawn from the past (supposing that they exist) will come straight out of an examination of the *facts,* viz. desires which have been realized. As if the desires which have not been realized were not as important, and perhaps more important, if you reflect that they may quite well come to fill the world's stage now.[2] Let me add

[1] See Note M at the end of this book.

[2] "A truly scientific mind," says one of these devotees of fact, "feels no need to justify a privilege which appears as an elementary and irreducible datum of the social world." (Paul Bourget.) But this same "truly scientific" mind is scandalized at an *insurrection* against this privilege, which is also an "elementary and irreducible datum of the social world." I shall be told this that insurrection is not a datum of the social world, but of the world of passion where it is most anti-social. And that indeed is the position of this dogmatism: It considers the social *independent of the passionate,* whether the latter has been made social (by Catholic education), or has been reduced to silence by force (school of Maurras) or by skill (school of Bainville). The strangest part of it all is that those who argue in this way about the social *in itself* accuse their adversaries of dealing in abstractions.

that this cult of fact also claims to be the sole discoverer of "the meaning of history" and "the philosophy of history," which there again shows a weakness of mind from which the preceding ages seem to have been free. When Bossuet and Hegel built up philosophies of history they were certainly no more metaphysicians than Taine or Comte or any of their noisy disciples, but at least they knew that they were so, that they could not be otherwise, and were not so naïve as to think themselves "pure scientists."

(c) The assertion that political forms should be adapted to "man as he is and always will be" (viz. unsocial and bloody, therefore eternally needing systems of coercion and military institutions). This effort of so many modern teachers to assert the imperfectibility of human nature appears as one of their strangest attitudes, if you realize that it tends towards nothing less than asserting the complete uselessness of their function, and proving that they have completely ceased to realize its very essence. When we see moralists, educators, professional providers of spiritual guidance, assert at the spectacle of human barbarism that "man is thus," that "he must be taken thus," that "you will never change him," we are tempted to ask them what is their reason for existing. And when we hear them reply that "they are positive minds and not Utopians," that "they are concerned with what is,

not with what might be," we are staggered to see
that they do not know that the moralist is essentially a Utopian, and that the nature of moral
action is precisely that it creates its object by affirming it. But we recover when we notice that
they are in no wise ignorant of this, and know
perfectly well that by affirming it they will create
that eternity of barbarism necessary to the maintenance of the institutions which are dear to them.[1]

The dogma of the incurable wickedness of man
has another root among some who profess it. This
is a Romantic pleasure in picturing the human race
as walled in by an inevitable and eternal woe. From
this point of view we may say that there has grown
up among certain political writers of our time a
real *Romanticism of Pessimism,* as false in its
absoluteness as the Optimism of Rousseau and
Michelet, in hatred of whom it has arisen, while
its haughty and so-called scientific attitude is most
impressive to simple souls.[2] This doctrine has un-

---

[1] The position I am here denouncing has nothing in common with that of a recent school of moralists (Rauh, Lévy-
Bruhl) who also desire "to take man as he is," but in order to
discover how he may be made better.

[2] This pessimism, whatever some of its heralds may say, has
nothing in common with the pessimism of the masters of the
seventeenth century. La Fontaine and La Bruyère attribute
nothing inevitable or eternal to the ills they portray. Let me
also point out that in their efforts to discourage hope, the
Romantics of Pessimism cannot claim (as M. Georges Goyau
has pointed out to them) that they are based on Catholic
tradition.

doubtedly borne fruits outside the world of literature, and at its voice there has arisen a humanity
which believes in nothing but its egotisms and
merely laughs at the naïve persons who still think
that it might become better. The modern "clerk"
has accomplished a truly new work—he has taught
man to deny his divinity. The import of such a
work is obvious. The Stoics claimed that pain is
abolished if it is denied; the thing is disputable in
the matter of pain, but it is absolutely true in the
matter of moral perfectibility.

I shall point out two more teachings inspired in
the modern "clerks," by their preaching of the
"strong State," and it will not be necessary to add
that they are new in the ministers of the spiritual:—

The first is the teaching whereby they declare to
Man that he is great to the extent that he strives
to act and to think as his ancestors, his race, his
environment thought, and ignores "individualism."
Thirty years ago many of the French teachers
hurled anathemas against the man who "claimed
to seek truth for himself," to arrive at his own
opinion, instead of adopting the opinion of his
nation which had been told what it ought to think
by its vigilant leaders. Our age has seen priests
of the mind teaching that the gregarious is the
praiseworthy form of thought, and that independent thought is contemptible. It is moreover cer-

tain that a group which desires to be strong has no use for the man who claims to think for himself.[1]

The second is the teaching whereby they declare to men that the fact that a group is numerous constitutes a right. This is the morality which the over-populated nations hear from many of their thinkers, while the other nations hear from many of theirs that if their low birth-rate continues they will become the objects of a "legitimate" extermination. The rights of numerousness admitted by men who claim to belong to the life of the mind —that is what modern humanity sees. But it is certain that if a nation is to be strong, it must be numerous.

This cult of the strong State and the moral methods which ensure it have been preached to mankind by the "clerks" far beyond the domain of politics, and on a wholly general plane. This is the preaching of *Pragmatism* whose teaching during the past fifty years by nearly all the influential moralists of Europe is one of the most remarkable turning points in the moral history of the human species. It is impossible to exaggerate the importance of a movement whereby those who for twenty centuries

---

[1] Such a group logically comes to declarations like the following, which every supporter of "integral nationalism" is bound to admire: "From to-night onwards let there be an end to the silly Utopia where every one thinks with his own head." (Impero, 4th November, 1926.) See Note N at the end of this volume.

taught Man that the criterion of the morality of an act is its disinterestedness, that good is a decree of his reason insofar as it is universal, that his will is only moral if it seeks its law outside its objects, should begin to teach him that the moral act is the act whereby he secures his existence against an environment which disputes it, that his will is moral insofar as it is a will "to power," that the part of his soul which determines what is good is its "will to live" wherein it is most "hostile to all reason," that the morality of an act is measured by its adaptation to its end, and that the only morality is the morality of circumstances. The educators of the human mind now take sides with Callicles against Socrates, a revolution which I dare to say seems to me more important than all political upheavals.[1]

I should like to point out certain particularly remarkable aspects of this preaching, which are probably not sufficiently realized.

[1] On Pragmatism, especially Nietzschean pragmatism, and the place it holds (whether they confess it or not) in almost all the moral and political teachings really characteristic of this time, see R. Berthelot, *Un Romantisme Utilitaire*, tome i, page 28 onwards. I can best show the novelty of the pragmatist attitude, especially among the French moralists, by quoting a remark of Montaigne which they all, before Barrès, would have ratified: "The honour and beauty of an action cannot be argued from its utility." Let us not forget, however, that Nietzsche, always unfaithful to his disciples, declares that "in the long run, utility, like everything else, is simply a figment of our imagination, and may well be the *fatal stupidity by which we shall one day perish.*"

I said that the modern "clerks" teach man that his desires are moral insofar as they tend to secure his existence at the expense of an environment which disputes it. In particular they teach him that his species is sacred insofar as it is able to assert its existence at the expense of the surrounding world.[1] In other words, the old morality told Man that he is divine to the extent that he becomes one with the universe; the new morality tells him that he is divine to the extent that he is in opposition to it. The former exhorted him not to set himself in Nature "like an empire within an empire"; the latter exhorts him to say with the fallen angels of Holy Writ, "We desire now to feel conscious of ourselves in ourselves, and not in God." The former, like the master of the *Contemplations,* said: "Believe, but not in ourselves"; the latter replies with Nietzsche and Maurras: "Believe, and believe in ourselves, only ourselves."

Nevertheless, the real originality of Pragmatism is not in that. Christianity exhorted man to set himself up against Nature, but did so in the name of his spiritual and disinterested attributes: Pragmatism exhorts him to do so in the name of his practical attributes. Formerly man was divine because he had been able to acquire the concept of justice, the idea of law, the sense of God; to-day he

---

[1] That is why Pragmatism is also called Humanism. (See F. Schiller, *Protagoras or Plato.*)

is divine because he has been able to create an equipment which makes him the master of matter. (See the glorifications of the *homo faber* by Nietzsche, Sorel, Bergson.)

Moreover, the modern "clerks" extol Christianity insofar as it is supposed to have been pre-eminently a school of practical, creative virtues, adjusted to the support of the great human institutions. This amazing deformation of a doctrine which in its precepts is so obviously devoted to the love of the spiritual alone, is not only taught by laymen, who are quite within their rights in trying to place their practical desires under the patronage of the highest moral authorities; it is also professed by the ministers of Jesus themselves. Pragmatist Christianity, as I mean it here, is preached to-day from all Christian pulpits.[1]

This exhortation to concrete advantages and to that form of soul which procures them, is expressed by the modern "clerk" in another very remarkable teaching: By praise of the military life and the feelings which go with it, and by contempt for civil life and the morality it implies. We know the doctrine preached in Europe during the past fifty years by its most esteemed moralists, their apology for war "which purifies," their veneration

[1] We know how the two are reconciled. Jesus, they say, preached the spirit of sacrifice, which is the basis of all human institutions. As if Jesus preached the spirit of sacrifice which wins battles and secures empires!

for the man of arms "the archtype of moral beauty," their proclamation of the supreme morality of "violence" or of those who settle their differences by duels and not before a jury, while they declare that respect for contracts is the "weapon of the weak," the need for justice the "characteristic of slaves." It is not betraying the disciples of Nietzsche or Sorel—that is, the great majority of contemporary men of letters who attempt to set up a scale of moral values for the world—to say that according to them Colleoni is a far superior specimen of humanity to l'Hôpital. The estimates of the *Voyage du Condottiere* are not peculiar to the author of that work. Here is an idealization of practical activity, which humanity had never before heard from its educators, at least from those who speak dogmatically.

I shall be told that Nietzsche and his school do not extol the military life because it procures material advantages, but on the contrary, because it is the type of disinterested realism, and in opposition to the realism which in their opinion is the characteristic of civilian life. Yet it is none the less true that the way of life praised by these moralists is in fact that which preëminently brings material advantages. Whatever may be said by the author of *Reflections on Violence* and his disciples, war is more profitable than the counting house; to take is more advantageous than to exchange; Colleoni possesses more than Franklin. (Naturally, I am speaking of the successful military man, since Nietzsche and Sorel never speak of the merchant who goes bankrupt.)

Moreover, no one will deny that the irrational activities, of which the military instinct is only one aspect, are extolled by their great modern apostles for their practical value. Their historian has put it admirably: The Romanticism of Nietzsche, Sorel, and Bergson is a *utilitarian* Romanticism.

Let me insist that what I am pointing to here, is not the modern "clerk's" extolling of the military spirit, but of the warlike instinct. It is the cult of the warlike instinct, outside all social spirit of discipline or sacrifice which is meant by the following assertions of Nietzsche, glorified by a French moralist whom himself has numerous followers:—

"The values of the warrior aristocracy are founded on a powerful bodily constitution, excellent health, without forgetting all that is necessary to the upkeep of that overflowing vigour—war, adventure, hunting, dancing, physical games and exercises, and in general everything which implies a robust, free and joyous activity."

"That audacity of noble races, a mad, absurd, spontaneous audacity . . . their indifference and scorn for all safety of body, for life, comfort . . ."

"The superb blond beast wandering in search of prey and carnage . . ."

"The terrible gaiety and profound joy felt by heroes in all destruction, in all the pleasures of victory and cruelty."

The moralist who quotes those remarks (Sorel, *Reflexions sur la Violence*, p. 360) adds, in order to leave no doubt about his recommendation of them to his fellow human beings: "It is quite evident that liberty would be seriously compromised if men came to look upon the Homeric values" (which, for him, are the values just praised by Nietzsche) "as being characteristic of the barbarous peoples only."

Is it necessary to observe how, here again, the moral presentation dominant among the world's educators is essentially Germanic, and shows the bankruptcy of Graeco-Roman thought? Before our times you do not find in France a single serious moralist (including de Maistre) or even a poet (if you consider only the great ones) who praises the "pleasures of victory and cruelty." [1] And it is the same for ancient Rome, among the nations to whom war had given world supremacy. I do not find a single passage which puts forward the instincts of prey as the supreme form of human morality in Cicero, Seneca, or Tacitus, or even in Virgil, Ovid, Lucan, and Claudian. On the other hand, I find a great many which attribute this rank

[1] "The true warrior remains human in the midst of the blood he sheds." (De Maistre.)

to the instincts on which civil life is based.[1] More-over, in primitive Greece, long before the philos-ophers, the myths very soon give an important place to civil morality. In a poem of Hesiod the tomb of Cycnus is engulfed in the waters by Apollo's command, because Cycnus was a brigand. The defense of warlike instincts by Mediterranean moralists will be one of the amazements of history. Some of them, moreover, seem uneasy about it, and feel they ought to claim that the Homeric values (we have seen what they mean by that) "are very close to the values of Corneille" [2]—as if the French poet's heroes, with all their sense of devotion to duty and the State, had anything in common with lovers of adventure, prey, and carnage!

It will be observed that these passages from Nietzsche praise the military life apart from any political aim.[3] And, in fact, the modern "clerks" teach men that war implies a morality *in itself* and should be exercised even apart from any utility. This thesis, so familiar in Barrès, has been defended in its full splendor by a young hero who is an edu-

---

[1] For example, when they make a soldier say in heaven: "You must know, my friends, that among all things done upon earth, nothing is more agreeable to the eyes of those who rule the universe than societies of men founded upon respect for laws, which we call cities." (Cicero, *Scipio's Dream.*)

[2] Sorel, loc. cit.

[3] And from any patriotism. Nietzsche and Sorel prove that love of war is something totally distinct from love of country, although most often they coincide.

cator of the soul for a whole French generation:
"In my country we love war and secretly desire it. We have always made war. Not to conquer a province, not to exterminate a nation, not to settle a conflict of interests. . . . We make war for the sake of making war, with no other purpose." [1]

The old French moralists, even the soldiers (Vauvenargues, Vigny), looked upon war as a sad necessity; their descendants recommend it as a noble inutility. Yet, here again, the cult preached as apart from the practical and as an art happens to be eminently favorable to the practical—useless war is the best preparation for useful war.

This teaching leads the modern "clerk" (we have just seen it in Nietzsche) to confer a *moral* value upon physical exercise and to proclaim *the morality of sport*—a most remarkable thing indeed among

---

[1] Ernest Psichari, *Terres de Soleil et de Sommeil.* And, in *L'Appel des armes,* through the mouth of a character who obviously has all the author's sympathies; "I think it necessary that there should be in the world a certain number of the men who are called soldiers and who place their ideal in fighting, who have a taste for battle, not for victory but for the contest, as hunters have a taste for hunting, not for game! . . . The part we have to play, or otherwise we lose our reason for existing and have no more meaning, is to maintain a military ideal, not a nationally military ideal, but a militarily military ideal, if I may so express it." The religion of this moralist is, according to his own expression, *integral militarism.* "Big guns," he says, "are the most real realities which exist, the sole realities of the modern world." And obviously these realities are divinities for this "spiritual" person and his followers.

those who for twenty centuries have exhorted man to situate good in states of the mind. The moralists of sport, moreover, do not all shuffle over the practical essence of their doctrine. Young people, Barrès clearly teaches, should be trained in physical strength, for the greatness of the country. The modern educator goes for his inspiration, not to those who strolled in the Lyceum or to the solitaries of Clairvaux, but to the founder of a little town in the Peloponnesus. Moreover, our age has seen this new thing: Men who claim to belong to the spiritual life teaching that the Greece to venerate is Sparta with her gymnasiums, not the city of Plato or Praxiteles, while others maintain that in antiquity we should honor Rome and not Greece. All these things are perfectly consistent in those who desire to preach to humanity nothing but strong constitutions and solid ramparts.[1]

[1] This depreciation of Greece, to be seen in many French traditionalists since de Maistre, is constant among the Pangermanists. (See notably Houston Chamberlain, *Genesis of the Nineteenth Century*, tome i, page 57.) In a periodical with dogmatic claims (*Notre Temps*, August, 1927), under the suggestive title "Towards a Practical Idealism," I read: "A young generation trained in this way, *more sporting than ideological*, supports those who ask whether we are not at the dawn of a great age." Here again the Churchmen do not lag behind. In *La Vie Catholique* (24th September, 1927) I find a warm eulogy of a champion boxer. It is true that this eulogy ends up with the words: "Finally, let us add that Tunney is a convinced and practicing Catholic, and that two of his sisters are nuns."

The preaching of realism leads the modern "Clerk" to certain teachings, whose novelty in his history is not sufficiently noticed, nor what a break they form with the teaching which his class has given to men for the past two thousand years.

(a) *The extolling of courage,* or more precisely the exhortation to make the supreme virtue Man's aptitude to face death, while all other virtues, however lofty, are placed below it. This teaching, openly the teaching of Nietzsche, Sorel, Péguy, Barrès, was always the teaching of poets and generals, but is entirely new among the "clerks," I mean among men who put before the world a scale of values in the name of philosophical reflection, or who are willing to be considered as such. From Socrates to Renan they had considered courage as a virtue, but on a lower plane. All, more or less openly, teach with Plato: "In the first rank of virtue are wisdom and temperance; courage only comes afterwards."[1] The impulses they exhort

[1] Laws, Book I. The exact text of Plato is: "In the order of virtues, wisdom is first, temperance comes next, courage occupies the last place." Plato here means by courage (see the context, notably the passage about those soldiers who "though insolent, unjust, immoral, know how to fight") Man's aptitude for facing death. It seems that he would not have given the first place to the courage which is strength of mind, a resistance to misfortune, as the Stoics afterwards did. With him strength of mind always comes after justice—according to his doctrine, it is a consequence of justice. Moreover, the courage placed in the supreme rank by Barrès is not Stoic patience but the active defiance of death. For Nietzsche and

man to venerate are not those whereby he strives
to quench his thirst for placing himself in the real,
but those whereby he moderates it. It was reserved
for our time to see the priests of the spiritual placing in the first rank of forms of soul that which is
indispensable to man if he is to conquer and to lay
foundations.[1] However, this practical value of
courage, plainly expressed by Nietzsche and Sorel,
is not equally so expressed by all the modern moralists who praise this virtue. This brings another
of their teachings before us:—

Sorel it is essential audacity, where audacity is irrational—a
form of courage depreciated by all ancient moralists and their
disciples. (See Plato, Laches; Aristotle, Ethics, VIII; Spinoza,
Ethics, IV, 69; even the poets—"Our reason which commands
our fire," Ronsard.)

It seems that facing death, even on behalf of justice, was
not so much the object of praise among the ancient philosophers as it is among the moderns. In the Phaedo, Socrates is
praised for his justice; he is not very loudly praised because
he died for justice. Moreover, the views of the ancients on
this point seem to me well expressed by Spinoza: "Death is a
thing of which the free man thinks least of all," a thought
which does not imply much admiration for those who face
death bravely. One wonders whether the veneration of courage, at least among the moralists, has not been created by
Christianity, with the importance it attaches to death, and the
subsequent appearance before God.

I cannot leave this point without recalling a passage where
Saint-Simon speaks of a nobility "accustomed to be good for
nothing except to get itself killed," Memoires, t. xi, page 427,
ed. Cheruel. It may be asserted that there is not one modern
writer, even a Duke of France, who would speak of courage
in such a tone.

[1] And to hold.

(*b*) *The extolling of honor,* by which is meant all those impulses which cause a man to risk his life for no practical interest—to be precise, from desire of glory—*but which are an excellent school of practical courage,* and were always extolled by those who lead men to the conquest of material things. In this connection, let the reader think of the respect in which the institution of the duel has always been held in armies, in spite of certain repressions inspired solely by practical considerations.[1]

Here again, the position attributed to these impulses by so many modern moralists is something new among them, especially in the country of Montaigne, Pascal, La Bruyère, Montesquieu, Voltaire and Renan, who, when they extol honor, mean something very different from man's cult of his own glory.[2] Nevertheless, the most remarkable thing about all this is that the cult of man for his

[1] There will be found in Barrès (*Une Enquête aux pays du Levant,* chap. vii: "Les derniers fidèles du Vieux de la Montagne") a striking example of admiration for the cult of honor inasmuch as this cult, when ably exploited by an intelligent leader, gives practical results.

[2] This is especially the case with Montaigne who, as every one knows, extols honor insofar as it is man's sensitiveness to the judgment of his conscience, but very little insofar as it is a desire for glory—"put off with other pleasures that which comes from the approbation of others." Barrès believes he sees in that "a foreigner who does not share our prejudices." Barrès confuses the moralists and the poets. Before him I do not know one French author with dogmatic claims who has attributed a high moral value to the love of glory; the French

own glory is currently preached by the Churchmen as a virtue which leads Man to God. Is it not
amazing to hear words like the following from a
Christian pulpit? "The love of grandeurs is the
path to God, and the heroic impulse which fully
coincides with the search for glories in their cause,
permits him who had forgotten God or who
thought he knew not God to re-invent Him, to
discover this last summit after temporary ascents
have rendered him accustomed to the dizziness and
air of altitudes." [1] One cannot forbear quoting

moralists before 1890 are very unmilitary, even the soldiers
like Vauvenargues and Vigny. (See the excellent study of
G. Le Bidois, *L'Honneur au miroir de nos lettres,* especially on
Montesquieu.)

[1] The Abbé Sertillanges, *L'Héroisme et la Gloire.* Compare
this with Bossuet's two sermons on "The Honour of the
World." You can measure the advance made by the Church
during three centuries in its concessions to lay passions. See
also Nicole: "On the true idea of valour." The sermons of the
Abbé Sertillanges ("la Vie Héroïque") should be read entire,
as a monument of a Churchman's enthusiasm for warlike instincts. It is positively the manifesto of a helmed "clerk."
You can find in them such emotions as the following which,
mutatis mutandis, might be an extract from the Regimental
Orders of a Colonel of the Death's Head Hussars: "Behold
Guynemer, the young hero, the simple soul with the eagle
glance, the slim Hercules, the Achilles who does not retire
to his tent, the Roland of the clouds and the Cid of the
French sky: was there ever a wilder and more furious paladin,
more careless of death whether his own or that of an enemy?
This "kid," as his comrades called him, only enjoyed the savage pleasure of attack, of the hard fight, of the clear victory,
and in him the arrogance of the conqueror was at once
charming and terrible."

the lesson given by a true disciple of Jesus to a Christian teacher who had also strangely forgotten his Master's word:—

"Have you noticed that the eight Beatitudes, the Sermon on the Mount, the Gospels, the whole of primitive Christian literature, contain not one word which sets military virtues among those which lead to the Kingdom of Heaven?" (Renan, *First Letter to Strauss*.) [1]

Let me observe that I am not reproaching the Christian preacher for giving their due to glory and other earthly passions, I am only reproaching him for trying to pretend that he is in harmony with his institution when he does so. We do not ask that the Christian shall not violate the Christian law; we only ask him to know that he is breaking it when he does break it. This seems to me admirably brought out by the remark of Cardinal Lavigerie who was asked: "What would you do, Eminence, if some one slapped your right cheek?" and who replied, "I know what I ought to do, but I do not know what I should do." *I know what I ought to do,* and therefore what I ought to teach. A man who speaks in that way may give way to every

[1] Let me recall Thomas Aquinas's definition of honor, which is not exactly the definition of the honor extolled by the Abbé Sertillanges: "Honour is good (like the love of human glory) on condition that charity is its principle, and the love of God or the good of one's neighbor is its object."

species of violence, and yet maintain Christian morality. Here actions are nothing; the judgment on the actions is everything.

Must I repeat that I am not deploring the fact that the cults of honor and courage should be preached to human beings; I am deploring the fact that they are preached *by the "clerks."* Civilization, I repeat, seems to me possible only if humanity consents to a division of functions, if side by side with those who carry out the lay passions and extol the virtues serviceable to them there exists a class of men who depreciate these passions and glorify the advantages which are beyond the material. What I think serious is that this class of men should cease to perform their office, and that those whose duty was to quench human pride should extol the same impulses of soul as the leaders of armies.

I shall be told that this preaching is imposed on the "clerks," at least in war-time, by the laymen, by the States, who to-day intend to mobilize all the moral resources of the nation for their ends.[1] But what amazes me is not so much that I see the "clerks" preaching in this manner, as to see them do it with such docility, such absence of disgust, such enthusiasm, such joy. . . . The truth is that

[1] See the recent Bill to amend Martial Law, known as the Paul Boncour Bill.

the "clerks" have become as much laymen as the laymen themselves.

(c) *The extolling of harshness* and the scorn for human love—pity, charity, benevolence. Here again, the modern "clerks" are the *moralists* of realism. They are not content to remind the world that harshness is necessary in order "to succeed" and that charity is an encumbrance, nor have they limited themselves to preaching to their nation or party what Zarathustra preached to his disciples: "Be hard, be pitiless, and in this way dominate." They proclaim the moral nobility of harshness and the ignominy of charity. This teaching, which is the foundation of Nietzsche's work, need not surprise one in a country which has not provided the world with a single great apostle,[1] but it is very remarkable in the land of Vincent de Paul and the defender of the Calas. Lines like the following, which might be an extract from the *Genealogy of Morals,* seem to me something wholly new coming from the pen of a French moralist: "This perverted pity has degraded love.[2] It has been given the name of charity, and the weak have received its dew. Night after night the seed of this calamity has been scattered. It conquers the earth. It fills

---

[1] This suggestive remark is Lavisse's, *Etudes d'Histoire de Prusse,* page 30. See the whole passage.

[2] Love here is obviously love for the superior species—to which the preacher naturally belongs. Doubtless it is this love also which permits of a pity which is not "perverted."

the solitary places. In whatever country you go, you cannot go about for a single day without meeting this withered face with its commonplace gestures, inspired by the sole desire of prolonging its shameful life."[1] There again we can observe how the modern realists have advanced beyond their predecessors. When Machiavelli declares that "a Prince in order to maintain his power is forced to govern in a manner contrary to charity and humanity," he is simply saying that to act contrary to charity may be a practical necessity, but he does not in the least touch that charity is a degradation of the soul. This teaching is the contribution of the nineteenth century to the moral education of mankind.

Sometimes the modern "clerks" claim that in preaching inhumanity they are only continuing the teaching of their great ancestors, particularly of Spinoza on acount of his famous proposition: "Pity in itself is bad and useless in a soul which lives according to reason." Is it necessary to point out that here pity is depreciated, not to the benefit of inhumanity, but to the benefit of humanity *guided by reason*, because reason alone "enables us to give

---

[1] Charles Maurras, *Action Française*, tome iv, page 596. One thinks of Nietzsche's exclamation: "Humanity! Was there ever a more horrible old woman among all horrible old women!" and the German master adds, always in agreement with many a French master as we shall see later, "unless perhaps it is truth."

aid to others with certainty." And Spinoza, determined to stress the fact that for him pity is only inferior to reasoned kindness, adds: "It must be fully understood that I am here speaking of the man who lives by reason. For if a man is never led by reason or by pity to go to the assistance of others, then assuredly he deserves the name of inhuman, since he retains no resemblance to a man." Let me add that the apostles of harshness cannot claim either that they are supported by the fanatics of justice (Michelet, Proudhon, Renouvier) who, by sacrificing love to justice, do perhaps end up in harshness, but not in a joyous harshness which is precisely the harshness preached by the modern realists, who say—perhaps rightly—that it is the only fertile kind.[1]

This extolling of harshness seems to me to have borne more fruit than any other preaching by the modern "clerks." It is a commonplace that among the great majority of the (so-called) thinking young men, in France for instance, harshness is to-day an object of respect, while human love in all its forms is considered a rather laughable thing. These young men have a cult for doctrines which respect nothing but force, pay no attention to the

[1] Their harshness has obviously nothing in common with the harshness implied by these fine words: "The man of justice subordinates passion to reason, which seems regrettable if his heart is cold, but will appear sublime if he is capable of love" (Renouvier).

142

lamentations of suffering and proclaim the inevitability of war and slavery, while they despise those who are revolted by such prospects and desire to alter them. I should like these cults to be compared with the literary esthetics of these young men, their veneration for certain contemporary novelists and poets in whom the absence of human sympathy reaches a rare pitch of perfection, and whom they plainly venerate, especially for that characteristic. And I should like you to observe the gloomy gravity and arrogance with which these young men subscribe to these "iron" doctrines. It seems to me that the modern "clerks" have created in so-called cultivated society a positive *Romanticism of harshness.*

They have also created a *Romanticism of contempt,* at least in France, and notably with Barrès, and indeed since Flaubert and Baudelaire. Nevertheless, it seems to me that in recent times contempt has been practiced in France for reasons quite other than esthetic. These peoples have come to see that by feeling contempt for others they are not only obtaining the pleasure of a lofty attitude, but that when they are really expert in expressing contempt they harm what they despise, do it a real damage. And in fact the kind of contempt which Barrès expresses for the Jews and which certain royalist teachers have displayed for democratic institutions every morning for the past twenty years, do really

143

harm their victims, at least among those very numerous artistic minds for whom a superbly executory gesture is as good as an argument. The modern "clerks" deserve a place of honor in the history of realism; they have come to understand the practical value of contempt.

It may also be said that they have created a *cult for cruelty*. Nietzsche proclaims that "every superior culture is built up on cruelty," a doctrine which is explicitly proclaimed in many places by Barrès, author of *Du sang, de la volupté et de la mort*. Nevertheless, the cult of cruelty, which may also be thought necessary "to succeed" [1] has remained limited to a few particularly artistic sensibilities, at least in France. It is very far from becoming the cult of a school, like harshness and contempt. Here again we may notice how new this cult is in the land of those who said "Cowardice, the mother of cruelty" (Montaigne), or, to quote a military moralist, "a hero does not feel proud of carrying hunger and misery among foreigners, but of enduring them for the State; nor of giving death, but of risking it." (Vauvenargues.) [2]

[1] This is the opinion of Machiavelli (chap. xviii) who, there again, does not therefore consider cruelty as a proof of a high state of culture.

[2] I find this from the pen of a hero of the First Empire: "I was afraid of feeling *pleasure*" (the author himself underlines the word) "in killing with my own hand some of these

(d) *The cult of success,* I mean the teaching which says that when a will is successful that fact alone gives it a moral value, whereas the will which fails is for that reason alone deserving of contempt. This philosophy which is professed by many a modern teacher in political life (it may be said, by all in Germany since Hegel, and by a large number in France since de Maistre) is also professed in private life, and has borne its fruits there. In the so-called thinking world to-day there are innumerable people who think they are demonstrating their aristocratic morality by declaring their systematic esteem for all who "succeed" and their scorn for all who fail. One moralist places to the credit of Napoleon's greatness of soul his contempt for "the unlucky"; others do the same thing in regard to Mazarin, Vauban, Mussolini. It cannot be denied that the "clerks" are thereby keeping an excellent school of realism, since the cult of success and the contempt for misfortune are obviously admirable moral conditions for obtaining material advantages. Nor can it be denied that this teaching is entirely

scoundrels" (he is speaking of some Germans who murdered French prisoners after the battle of Leipzic). "I therefore sheathed my sabre and left the extermination of these assassins to the troopers." (*Memoirs of General Marbot,* tome iii, page 344.) There is a condemnation of the joy of killing which would be scorned by many a contemporary writer. In France the glorification of warlike instincts is much less common among the soldiers than among the authors. Marbot is far less bloody-minded than Barrès.

new among them, especially among the "clerks" of the Latin races, I mean those whose ancestors had taught mankind to honor merit apart from its achievements, to honor Hector as much as Achilles, the Curiatii more than their successful rivals.[1]

We have just seen that the modern moralists extol the warrior at the expense of the man of justice. They also extol him at the expense of the man of learning and, there again, they preach to the world the cult of practical activity in defiance of the disinterested life. We all know Nietzsche's hue and cry against the man of the study, the man of erudition, "the mirror man," whose only passion is to understand. And also Nietzsche's esteem for the life of the mind solely insofar as it is emotion, lyricism, action, partiality; his derisive laughter at "objective" methodical research devoted to "the horrible old woman known as truth." And we know Sorel's denunciations of societies which "give a privileged place to the amateurs of *purely intellectual things*[2] (those of Barrès, Lemaître,

---

[1] "And the honour of virtue consists in contending, not in winning" (Montaigne).

[2] *La Ruine du monde antique*, page 76. See also in *Les Illusions du progrès* (page 259) Sorel's derisive amusement at a thinker who said that the preponderance of intellectual emotions is the sign of superior societies. We may take up Sainte-Beuve's famous distinction and say that modern thinkers extol *sword-intelligence* at the expense of *mirror-intelligence*. On their own showing it is the former they admire in Nietzsche, Sorel, Péguy, and Maurras. (See R. Gillouin, *Esquisses lit-*

Brunetière, thirty years ago, intimating to the "intellectuals" that they are a type of humanity "inferior to the soldier"; those of Péguy, who admires philosophies to the extent that "they are good fighters," and admires Descartes because he was in the army, and the dialecticians of French monarchism solely because they are ready to be killed for the sake of their views.[1] I shall be told that most often this is the mere wild talk of men of letters, the posturing of lyricists, to which it is unjust to attribute a dogmatic meaning; that Nietzsche, Barrès and Péguy denounce the life of study on account of their poetic temperaments, their aversion from everything lacking in picturesqueness and the spirit of adventure, and not their resolution to abase disinterestedness. To which I reply that these poets give themselves out as serious thinkers (notice their tone, *quite free from naïveté*); that the immense majority of their readers accept them as such; that, even if it were true that in depreciating the man of study their motive is not to abase disinterestedness, it is none the less true in fact that the manner of living they hold up to the laughter of mankind happens to be the

téraires et morales, page 52. Let me observe that contempt for "mirror-intelligence" implies contempt for Aristotle, Spinoza, Bacon, Goethe, and Renan. Nor does it seem to me that M. Paul Valéry is exactly a "sword-intelligence."

[1] *Victor Marie, Comte Hugo*, towards the end. See Note O at the end of this volume.

very type of the disinterested life, while the life
they extol at its expense is the very type of practical activity (at least more practical than that of
the man of study, for it will be admitted that the
activity of du Guesclin and Napoleon is more likely
to acquire material advantages than the activity
of Spinoza and Mabillon); that, moreover, what
these thinkers despise in the man of study is precisely the man who lays no foundations, who does
not conquer, who does not predicate the capture
of its environment by the species, or who, if he
does predicate it, as the scientist does by his discoveries, retains for himself only the joy of knowledge and abandons the practical exploitation of his
discoveries to others. In Nietzsche, the scorn for
the man of study to the benefit of the warrior is
only an episode in a desire which nobody will deny
inspires the whole of his work as well as the work
of Sorel, Barrès and Péguy: *The desire to abase the
values of knowledge before the values of action.*[1]

[1] This is the only reason why Nietzsche extols art, and declares (along with all modern moralism) the supremacy of the
artist over the philosopher, because art seems to him to possess
the value of action. Apart from this point of view, it seems
just to say with one of his critics: "At bottom Nietzsche
despised art and artists. . . . In art he condemns a feminine
principle, the mimicry of the actor, the love of dress and all
that glitters. . . . Remember the eloquent page where he
praises Shakespeare, the greatest of poets, for having abased
the figure of the poet, whom he treats as a stage-player, before

To-day this desire inspires not only the moralist, but another kind of "clerk" who speaks from much higher ground. I am referring to that teaching of modern metaphysics which exhorts man to feel comparatively little esteem for the truly thinking portion of himself and to honor the active and *willing* part of himself with all his devotion. The theory of knowledge from which humanity has taken its values during the past half century assigns a secondary rank to the mind which proceeds by clear and distinct ideas, by categories, by words, and places in the highest rank the mind which succeeds in liberating itself from these intellectual habits and in becoming conscious of itself insofar as it is a "pure tendency," a "pure will," a "pure activity." Philosophy which formerly raised man to feel conscious of himself because he was a thinking being and to say, "I think, therefore I am," now raises him to say, "I am, therefore I think," "I think, therefore I am not," (unless he takes thought into consideration only in that humble region where it is confused with action). Formerly philosophy taught him that his soul is divine insofar as it resembles the soul of Pythagoras linking up concepts; now she informs him that his soul is

Caesar, *that divine man."* (C. Schuwer, *Revue de Métaphysique et de Morale,* April, 1926.) For Sorel art is great because it is an anticipation of intense production, as it tends to manifest itself more and more in our society."

divine insofar as it resembles that of the small chicken breaking its eggshell.[1] From his loftiest pulpit the modern "clerk" assures man that he is great in proportion as he is practical.

During fifty years, especially in France (see Barrès and Bourget) a whole literature has assiduously proclaimed the superiority of instinct, the unconscious, intuition, the will (in the German sense, i.e. as opposed to the intelligence) and has proclaimed it in the name of the practical spirit, because the instinct and not the intelligence knows what we ought to do—as individuals, as a nation, as a class—to secure our own advantage. These writers have eagerly expatiated on the example of the insect whose "instinct" (it appears) teaches it to strike its prey precisely in the spot which will paralyze it without killing it, so that its offspring may feed on the living prey and develop better.[2]

[1] *Evolution Créatrice*, page 216. The true formula of Bergsonism should be, "I grow, therefore I am." Notice also the tendency of modern philosophy to make the practical character of thought its essential characteristic and to make its consciousness of itself a secondary characteristic: "Perhaps thought must be defined as the faculty of combining means towards certain ends rather than by the sole property of being clear to itself." (D. Roustan, *Leçons de Psychologie*, page 73.)

[2] The Sphex. The example is given in *L'Evolution Créatrice*, and has had an immense success in the literary world. (It is, moreover, imaginary. See Marie Goldsmith, *Psychologie Comparée*, page 211.) The defense of the practical value of instinct, with the same Romantic contempt of the rationalist as in Barrès, existed with J. J. Rousseau: "Conscience never

Other teachers denounce this "barbarous" extolling of instinct in the name of "the French tradition" and preach "the superiority of the intelligence"; but they preach it because in their opinion it is the intelligence which shows us the actions required by our interests, i.e. from exactly the same passion for the practical. This brings us to one of the most remarkable and certainly the most novel forms of this preaching of the practical by the modern "clerks."

I mean that teaching according to which *intellectual activity is worthy of esteem to the extent that it is practical and to that extent alone.* It may be said that since the Greeks the predominant attitude of thinkers towards intellectual activity was to glorify it insofar as (like esthetic activity) it finds its satisfaction in itself, apart from any attention to the advantages it may procure. Most thinkers would have agreed with Plato's famous hymn to geometry, where that discipline is venerated more than all others because for him it represents the type of speculative thought which brings in nothing material; and with Renan's verdict which declares that the man who loves science for its fruits commits the worst of blasphemies against that

deceives us; it is to the soul what instinct is to the body. . . . Modern philosophy, which only admits what can be explained, takes care not to admit the obscure faculty called instinct which, without acquired knowledge, seems to guide animals towards some end." (*Confession de foi du vicaire savoyard.*)

divinity.[1] By this standard of values the "clerks" put before the laymen the spectacle of a class of men for whom the value of life lies in its disinterestedness, and they acted as a check on—or at least shamed—the laymen's practical passions. The modern "clerks" have violently torn up this charter. They proclaim that intellectual functions are only respectable to the extent that they are bound up with the pursuit of a concrete advantage, and that the intelligence which takes no interest in its objects is a contemptible activity. They teach that the superior form of the intelligence is that which thrusts its roots into "the vital urge," occupied in discovering what is most valuable in securing our existence. In historical [2] science especially, they honor the intelligence which labors under the guidance of political interests,[3] and they are completely disdainful of all efforts towards "objectivity." Elsewhere they assert that the intelligence to be venerated is that which limits its activities within

[1] "If the utility which results from a man's occupations, determined our praise, the inventor of the plough would deserve the praise of being a great mind far more than Aristotle, Galilei, and M. Descartes." (Bayle.) Fontenelle and Voltaire have pointed out the utility of certain studies which were considered useless; they never meant that those who cultivated these studies while they thought them useless were therefore contemptible.

[2] See above, page 71.

[3] Or moral. Barrès denounces the "immorality" of the scholar who shows the part played by chance in history. Compare Michelet's remark, "respect kills history."

the bounds of national interests and social order, while the intelligence which allows itself to be guided by the desire for truth alone, apart from any concern with the demands of society, is merely a "savage and brutal" activity, which "dishonours the highest of human faculties." [1]   Let me also point out their devotion to the doctrine (Bergson, Sorel) which says that science has a purely utilitarian origin—the necessity of man to dominate matter, "knowledge is adaptation"; and their scorn for the beautiful Greek conception which made science

[1] As is well known, this is the argument of the "Avenir de l'Intelligence."   It allows followers to say ("Manifeste de l'Intelligence," *Figaro*, 19th July, 1919; on this manifesto, see Note P at the end of this volume) that "one of the most obvious missions of the Church during the ages has been to protect the intelligence against its own errors"—an irrefutable saying from the moment that the errors of the intelligence are everything it says without reference to social order (whose basis is to be the teaching of the Church).   This practical conception of the intelligence leads to definitions of this sort: "True logic is to be defined as the normal union of feelings, images and signs, to inspire in us the conceptions suited to our moral, intellectual and physical needs."   (Maurras.) Compare this with the tradition teaching of the French masters: "Logic is the art of guiding reason properly in the knowledge of things."   (*Logique de Port-Royal.*)

The wish to esteem intelligence according to its practical results appears again in this astounding formula: "A critical mind is of value *through the influence it exerts* by means of the enlightenment it bestows."   (Maurras.)   See also how severe is M. Massis (*Jugements*, i, 87) for Renan when he says: "The useful is what I abhor."   Elsewhere (*Jugements*, 107) the same thinker speaks of a spiritual freedom "whose disinterestedness is merely a refusal of the conditions of life, of action, *and of thought!*"

bloom from the desire to play, the perfect type of disinterested activity. And then they teach men that to accept an error which is of service to them (the "myth") is an undertaking which does them honor, while it is shameful to admit a truth which harms them. In other words, as Nietzsche, Barrès and Sorel plainly put it, sensibility to truth in itself apart from any practical aim is a somewhat contemptible form of mind.[1] Here the modern "clerk" positively displays genius in his defense of the material, since the material has nothing to do with the truth, or rather to speak more truly—has no worse enemy. The genius of Callicles in all its profundity lives again in the great masters of the modern soul.[2]

[1] They add "and unscientific," which is irrefutable as soon as science means "practical." "Bringing up children religiously," says M. Paul Bourget, "is bringing them up scientifically"—a very defensible saying as soon as "scientifically" means (as the author here wants it to mean) "in conformity with the national interest."

[2] The French traditionalists condemn the truth in itself in the name of "social" truth. This is the *glorification of prejudices,* a new thing indeed in the descendants of Montaigne and Voltaire. It may be said that certain contemporary French masters show a zeal in defending the interests of society never seen before in those whose business was to defend the interests of the mind.

The condemnation of disinterested intellectual activity is plainly laid down in this command of Barrès: "All questions must be solved in relation to France," to which a German thinker replies in 1920, "All the conquests of ancient and modern culture and of science are looked at by us from the German point of view before everything." (Quoted by C.

Then the modern "clerks" have preached to men the religion of the practical *by means of their theology*, through the image of God they have set before them. First, they determined that God, who since the Stoics has been infinite, should once more become finite, distinct, endowed with a personality, that He should be the affirmation of a *physical* and not a *metaphysical* existence. Anthropomorphism, which in the poets from Prudentius to Victor Hugo existed mingled with pantheism without troubling to define the frontiers between them, since God was personal or indeterminate according to the direction of the emotion and the needs of the lyric impulse, rose up in Péguy and Claudel with the most violent consciousness of itself, the clearest desire to be distinguished from its acolyte and to express contempt for him. At the same time the political teachers attacked the religion of the Infinite with a precision of hatred, a skill in depreciation, unparalleled even in the Church, which consisted in denouncing this religion precisely because it is not practical, because it saps away the feelings which found the great earthly realities: the City and the State.[1] But the modern

Chabot, Preface to the French translation of *Speeches to the German Nation*, page xix.) For the cult of the "useful error," see an amazing page in the *Jardin de Bérénice*, quoted and commented on by Parodi. (*Traditionalisme et Democratie*, page 136.)

[1] Here M. Maurras separates from his Master, de Maïstre,

"clerks" have above all endowed God with the attributes which secure practical advantages. It may be said that, since the Old Testament, God was far more just than strong, or rather that, as Plato thought, His strength was only a form of His justice; and His power, as Malebranche and Spinoza put it, had nothing in common with the power of kings and Empire-builders. The desire to increase was implicitly excluded from His nature, as well as the moral attributes necessary to the satisfaction of that desire—energy, will, the love of effort, the attraction of triumph. This was an inevitable result of His perfect and infinite state of being, which at once constituted the whole of possible reality. Even in creation, the idea of which is essentially inseparable from the ideas of power and increase, these ideas were avoided—the world was far less a result of God's power than of His love; it came out of God as a ray comes out of the sun, without God feeling any increase of Himself at the expense of anything else. God, to speak in terms of the schools, was far less the transcendent cause of the world than its immanent cause.[1] On the other

who speaks of "the ocean which will one day welcome everything and every one to its bosom." However, the author of the *Soirées de Saint-Petersbourg* quickly adds: "But I refrain from touching on personality, without which immortality is nothing."

[1] On the existence of this doctrine of immanence among almost all Christian teachers until our own times, see Renouvier: "L'Idée de Dieu" (*Année Philosophique*, 1897), and

hand, for the modern teachers (Hegel, Schelling, Bergson, Péguy), God is essentially something which increases; His law is "incessant change," "incessant novelty," "incessant [1] creation"; His principle is essentially a principle of growth—Will, Tension, Vital Urge. If He is Intelligence, as with Hegel, He is an intelligence which "develops," which "realizes itself" more and more. The Being situated immediately in all His perfection and knowing nothing of conquest is an object of contempt; He represents (Bergson) an "eternity of death." [2] So the believers in an initial and single creation to-day strive to present this act in its purely practical aspect. The Church condemns with a hitherto unknown clearness every doctrine of immanence and preaches transcendence in all its strictness.[3] God, in creating the world, no longer witnesses an inevitable expansion of His nature; through His power (some, to diminish the arbitrariness, say "through His benevolence") he

also *Essai d'une Classification des doctrines*, 3: *l'évolution; la création.*

[1] According to Hegel, God constantly grows at the expense of His opposite; His activity is essentially that of war and victory.

[2] Let me note a keen protest against this conception in "Neo-Thomism."

[3] Compare, for instance, the condemnation of Rosmini with that of Maître Eckart, where such propositions as "Nulla in Deo distinctio esse aut intelligi potest" and "Omnes creaturae sunt purum nihil" are declared to be, not heretical, but only "ill-sounding, rash and suspected of heresy."

sees the arising of something clearly distinct from Himself, something on which He sets His hand. His act, whatever may be said to the contrary, is the perfect model of material aggrandizement. Like the prophet of Israel of old, the modern "clerk" says to mankind: "Display your zeal for the Eternal, the God of battles."

For half a century, such has been the attitude of men whose function is to thwart the realism of nations, and who have labored to excite it with all their power and with complete decision of purpose. For this reason I dare to call this attitude "The Treason of the Intellectuals." If I look for its causes, I see profound causes which forbid me to look upon this movement as a mere fashion, to which the contrary movement might succeed to-morrow.

One of the principal causes is that the modern world has made the "clerk" into a citizen, subject to all the responsibilities of a citizen, and consequently to despise lay passions is far more difficult for him than for his predecessors. If he is reproached for not looking upon national quarrels with the noble serenity of Descartes and Goethe, the "clerk" may well retort that his nation claps a soldier's pack on his back if she is insulted, and crushes him with taxes even if she is victorious. If shame is cried upon him because he does not rise superior to social hatreds, he will point out that the

day of enlightened patronage is over, that to-day
he has to earn his living, and that it is not his fault
if he is eager to support the class which takes a
pleasure in his productions. No doubt this explanation is not valid for the true "clerk," who
submits to the laws of his State without allowing
them to injure his soul. He renders unto Caesar
the things that are Caesar's, i.e. his life perhaps, but
nothing more. The true "clerk" is Vauvenargues,
Lamarck, Fresnel, who never imbibed national
patriotism although they perfectly performed their
patriotic duty; he is Spinoza, Schiller, Baudelaire,
César Franck, who were never diverted from
single-hearted adoration of the Beautiful and the
Divine by the necessity of earning their daily bread.
But such "clerks" are inevitably rare. So much
contempt for suffering is not the law of human
nature even among the "clerks"; the law is that
the living creature condemned to struggle for life
turns to practical passions, and thence to the sanctifying of those passions. The "clerk's" new faith
is to a great extent a result of the social conditions
imposed upon him, and the real evil to deplore is
perhaps not so much the "great betrayal" of the
"clerks" as the disappearance of the "clerks," the
impossibility of leading the life of a "clerk" in the
world of to-day. One of the gravest responsibilities
of the modern State is that it has not maintained
(but could it do so?) a class of men exempt from

civic duties, men whose sole function is to maintain non-practical values. Renan's prophecy is verified; he foretold the inevitable degradation of a society where every member was forced to discharge worldly tasks, although Renan himself was the very type of those whom such servitude would never have prevented—in the phrase of one of his peers—"from breathing only in the direction of Heaven."

It would be very unjust to explain the existence of national passion in the modern "clerk" by self-interest alone. This is also to be explained, and in a more simple manner, by the love, the impulse which naturally inspires every man to love the group from which he derives, more than the other groups which share the earth. There again, it may be argued that the "clerk's" new faith is caused by the changes of the nineteenth century, which by giving national groups a consistency hitherto unknown furnishes food to a passion which in many countries before that period could have been little more than potential. Obviously, attachment to the world of the spirit alone was easier for those who were capable of it when there were no nations to love. And, in fact, it is most suggestive to notice that the true appearance of the "clerk" coincides with the fall of the Roman Empire, i.e. with the time when the great nation collapsed and the little nations had not yet come into existence. It is equally suggestive to notice that the age of the great lovers of spiritual things, the age of Thomas Aquinas, Roger Bacon, Galilei, Erasmus, was the age when most of Europe was in a state of chaos and the nations were unknown; that the regions where pure speculation endured longest seem to be Germany and Italy,[1] i.e. the regions which were the last to be nationalized; and practically ceased to produce pure speculation from the moment when they became nations. Of course, here again the vicissitudes of the world of sense do not affect the true "clerk." The misfortunes of their country, and even its triumphs, did not prevent Einstein and Nietzsche from feeling no passion but the passion for thought. When Jules Lemaître exclaimed that the wound of Sedan made him lose his reason, Renan replied that he perfectly retained his, and that a true priest of the mind could only be wounded in other than earthly interests.[2]

[1] Remember that in 1806, immediately after Jena, Hegel's one thought was to find a corner in which to philosophize. In 1813 Schopenhauer was completely indifferent to the up-rising of Germany against Napoleon.

[2] "No one has the right to be indifferent to the disasters of his country; but the philosopher, like the Christian, always has reasons for living. The Kingdom of God knows neither conquerors nor conquered; that Kingdom resides in the joys of the heart, the mind, and the imagination, which the conquered enjoys more than the conqueror if he is morally on a higher plane and has more mind. Your great Goethe, your admirable Fichte have taught us, have they not, how to lead

In the cases I have just mentioned, the "clerk's" devotion to his nation or class is sincere, whether it is from interest or from love. I admit I think this sincerity is infrequent. The practice of the life of the spirit seems to me to lead inevitably to universalism, to the feeling of the eternal, to a lack of vigor in the belief in worldly conventions. The sincerity of national passion especially, in men of letters particularly, seems to me to assume the virtue of naïveté, which every one will admit is not characteristic of this body of men, apart from their own self-esteem. It will also be hard to convince me that the motives of their public attitudes in artists are such simple things as the desire to live and to eat. I therefore seek—and find—other reasons for the realism of the modern "clerk," and these, although less natural, are none the less profound. They seem to me particularly valid for men of letters, especially in France, the country where the attitude of writers in the past half century differs most from that of their fathers.

First of all, I see the interests of their careers. It is an obvious fact that during the past two centuries most of the men of letters who have attained

a noble and consequently happy life, when our country is humiliated abroad." (First Letter to Strauss.)

Need I say that Nietzsche, who seems to me a bad "clerk" from the nature of his teaching, seems to me one of the finest from his entire devotion to the passions of the spirit alone?

wide fame in France assumed a political attitude—
for instance, Voltaire, Diderot, Chateaubriand,
Lamartine, Victor Hugo, Anatole France, Barrès.
With some of them, real fame dates from the moment when they assumed that attitude. This law
has not escaped the attention of their descendants,
and it may be said to-day that every French writer
who desires wide fame (which means every writer
endowed with the real temperament of a man of
letters) also desires inevitably to play a political
part. This desire may arise from other motives.
For instance, in Barrès and d'Annunzio, from the
desire "to act," to be something more than "men
at a desk," to lead a life like that of the "heroes"
and not like that of "scribes"; or, more ingenu-
ously, as no doubt happened with Renan when he
stood as a Parliamentary candidate, from the idea
that he could perform a public service. Let me add
that the modern writer's desire to be a political
man is excused by the fact that the position is to
some extent offered him by public opinion, whereas
the compatriots of Racine and La Bruyère would
have laughed in their faces if they had thought of
publishing their views on the advisability of the
war with Holland or the legality of Chambres de
réunion. There again, it was easier to be a true
"clerk" in the past than to-day.

These observations explain why the contempo-

rary French writer so frequently desires to assume
a political attitude, but they do not explain why
this attitude is so inevitably in support of arbitrary
authority.   Liberalism is also a political attitude;
and the least which can be said is that the modern
French "clerk" has very seldom adopted it in the
past twenty years. Another factor comes in here.
That is the practical writer's desire to please the
bourgeoisie, who are the creators of fame and the
source of honors. It may even be argued that for
this sort of writer the necessity to treat the passions of this class with deference is greater than
ever, if I may judge by the fate of those who in
recent times have dared to defy them, i.e. Zola,
Romain Rolland. Now, the bourgeoisie of to-day,
terrified by the progress of the opposing class,
solely anxious to retain the privileges which are
left them, feel nothing but aversion from liberal
dogmas; and the man of letters who displays any
political flag is bound to wave the flag of "Order"
if he wishes to obtain favors. The case of Barrès is
particularly instructive from this point of view.
He began as a great intellectual skeptic, and his
material star waxed a hundredfold greater, at least
in his own country, on the day when he made himself the apostle of "necessary prejudices." This
sort of thing makes me believe that the present
political fashion of French writers is going to last
a long time. A phenomenon which is caused by

the uneasiness of the French bourgeoisie does not seem likely to disappear quickly.[1]

I have mentioned the lot of those writers who in quite recent times have dared to thwart the passions of the bourgeoisie. This is only one aspect of a very general novelty, of supreme interest to the subject I am discussing. I mean the consciousness of their sovereignty felt by the herd of laymen, and the resolution they display to bring to his senses any writer who dares to say anything but what they wish to hear. This propensity of the layman appears not only in his relations with his writers (and with his press—a newspaper which does not supply its readers with the exact errors they cherish is immediately dropped), but, which is far more remarkable, in his relations with his truly "clerical" teachers, whose voice speaks to him in the name of the Divine. The pulpit-orator who really presumed to censure nationalist passion, who really mortified bourgeois arrogance, would soon (particularly in France) see his flock disperse. He can no longer terrify such a gathering with the fear of punishment, and they no longer believe in anything but the real; consequently they feel stronger and more important than he, and only consent to listen to his preaching on condition that he treats with

[1] Of course, I am not doubting the sincerity of all the "right-thinking" men of letters. Some persons are so fortunate that the most profitable attitudes are precisely those which they adopt sincerely.

165

deference—not to say sanctifies—the egotisms they venerate.[1] Modern humanity is fully determined that those who call themselves its teachers, shall be its servants and not its guides. And most of the teachers understand this admirably.[2]

To come back to the modern writer and the causes for his political attitude—I shall add that he is not only in the service of a bourgeoisie which is in a state of anxiety, but that he himself has become more and more of a bourgeois, endowed with all the social position and respect which belong to that caste. The Bohemian man of letters has practically disappeared, at least among those who engage public interest. Consequently, he has more and more come to possess the bourgeois form of soul, one of those most conspicuous characteristics

[1] This may be clearly seen by the ill-will displayed by the French bourgeoisie towards the order of their "spiritual leader" forbidding them to read a publication whose doctrines they like. The change may be estimated if you remember that when, a century ago, the Pope ordered the French Catholics to accept the law against the Jesuits voted by the government of Charles X, they all bowed to his will.

[2] At the end of the War of the Spanish Succession when the north of France was invaded, Fénelon delivered several sermons in which he told the invaded population that their sufferings were the just punishment for their sins. Imagine the reception of any one who dared to preach such a sermon to the French in August, 1914! For the manner in which the "taught" Church to-day treats the "teaching" Church if the latter does not say what it wants to hear, think of the reception thirty years ago of Father Ollivier's sermon on the victims of the fire at the charity bazaar.

is an affectation of the political feelings of the aristocracy—an attachment to systems of arbitrary authority, to military and priestly institutions, a scorn for societies founded upon justice, upon civic equality, a cult for the past, etc. . . . How many writers in France during the past fifty years, men whose names are on every one's lips, obviously think they are ennobling themselves by expressing disgust for democratic institutions! [1] In the same way I explain the adoption by many of them of harshness and cruelty, which they think are also attributes of the souls of the nobility.

The reasons I have just mentioned for the new political attitude of men of letters arise from the changes in their social status. Those I am about to mention arise from changes in the structure of their minds, in their literary desires, in their esthetic cults, in their morality. These reasons seem to me even more worthy of the historian's attention than those which have gone before.

First of all, we have their Romanticism, taking that word to mean the desire which arose in the writers of the nineteenth century (but which has

---

[1] Similar observations may be made about the philosophers, most of whom—and not the least famous—do not live to-day like Descartes and Spinoza, but are married, have children, occupy posts, are "in daily life." All of which seems to me to have a relation with the "pragmatic" character of their teaching. (On this point, see my book: *Sur le Succès du Bergsonisme*, page 207.)

become greatly perfected in the last thirty years)
to treat themes which lend themselves in a literary
manner to striking attitudes. About 1890 the
men of letters, especially in France and Italy, realized with astonishing astuteness that the doctrines
of arbitrary authority, discipline, tradition, contempt for the spirit of liberty, assertion of the
morality of war and slavery, were opportunities
for haughty and rigid poses infinitely more likely
to strike the imagination of simple souls than the
sentimentalities of Liberalism and Humanitarianism. And as a matter of fact, the so-called re-
actionary doctrines do lend themselves to a pessimistic and contemptuous Romanticism which
makes a far deeper impression on the common
herd than enthusiastic and optimistic Romanticism.
The pose of a Barrès or a d'Annunzio strikes naïve
persons far more than that of a Michelet or a
Proudhon. Moreover, these doctrines are to-day
given forth as founded upon science, upon "pure
experience," and thereby permit a tone of calm
inhumanity (the Romanticism of Positivism)
whose effect on the herd has not escaped the saga-
cious eye of the man of letters. (Of course, I am
only speaking of the elegant herd; Romantic pessimism has no value whatsoever for the people.)

There is another transformation of the literary
soul in men of letters, wherein I think I see a cause
of their new political creed. This is, that recently

the only one of their faculties they venerate is their artistic sensibility, on which to some extent they base all their judgments. Until the last thirty years it may be said that men of letters, at least in Latin Europe, disciples in this of the Greeks, were determined in their judgments—even their literary judgments—far more by their sensibility to reason than by their artistic sensibility, whereof moreover they were scarcely conscious as something distinct from the former. This remark is true for the men of the Renaissance and their direct descendants (the French writers of the seventeenth and succeeding century) and, despite appearances, it is also true of those who lived at the beginning of the nineteenth century. If the weakening of sensibility to reason and, more generally, of lofty intellectual discipline, is indisputably one of the characteristics of the Romanticism of 1830, the contempt for this sensibility makes no appearance. Victor Hugo, Lamartine, Michelet never prided themselves on despising the values of reason in things in order to esteem only their art values. Now, towards 1890, there occurred a revolution whose influence cannot be exaggerated. Enlightened by philosophical analysis (Bergsonism), the men of letters became conscious of the fundamental difference between intellectual sensibility and artistic sensibility; and ardently chose the latter. This is the epoch when they were heard to assert that a book is great as soon as it achieves a literary and artistic success, that its intellectual content is of no interest, that all arguments are equally defensible, that error is no more false than truth, etc.[1] This great change affected their political attitudes. Obviously, as soon as we think things are good only insofar as they content our artistic needs, the only good political systems are those of arbitrary authority. Artistic sensibility is far more gratified by a system which tends to the realization of force and grandeur than by a system which tends to the establishment of justice, for the characteristic of artistic sensibility is the love of concrete realities and the repugnance for abstract conceptions and conceptions of pure reason, the model of which is the idea of justice. Artistic sensibility is especially flattered by the spectacle of a mass of units which are subordinated to each other up to the final head who dominates them all, whereas the spectacle of a democracy, which is a mass of units *where no one is first,* deprives this sensibility of one of its fundamental needs.[2] Add to this that every doctrine

[1] This is the reign (which seems eternal in France) of the "wit," with his attribute so admirably denounced by Malebranche in this delicious phrase: "The stupid person and the wit are equally blind to truth; with this difference, that the stupid person respects truth while the wit despises it."

[2] The spectacle of democracies may satisfy another sort of artistic sensibility, i.e. the sort which is moved, not by the spectacle of order, but by the spectacle of an equilibrium between forces which are naturally in opposition. (On this

which honors Man in the universal, in what is common to all men, is a personal injury to the artist, whose characteristic (at least since Romanticism)[1] is precisely to set himself up as an exceptional being. Add also the sovereignty the artist now attributes to his desires and their satisfaction (the "rights of genius") and, consequently, his natural hatred for systems which limit each person's liberty of action by that of others. And finally add the artist's aversion from everything which is general, everything which is only the object of conception, not of sensation.[2] The determination of men of letters to pass judgment only in accordance with their artistic sensibility is only one aspect of their desire (since Romanticism) to exalt feeling at the expense of thought, a desire which itself is one among the thousand results of the decline of intel-

distinction, see the great book by M. Hauriou, *Principes de droit public*, chap. i.) Nevertheless, a sensibility to equilibrium is far more intellectual than truly artistic. See Note Q at the end of this book.

[1] More precisely, since the haughty Romanticism I mentioned above. The artist's desire to set himself up as an exceptional being dates from Flaubert. Hugo and Lamartine never expressed it.

[2] This aversion is particularly strong in Nietzsche. (See *Le Gai sçavoir,*" loc. cit., where generalization becomes a synonym for platitude, superficiality, stupidity.) Like a true artist, Nietzsche is incapable of understanding that the apperception of a common characteristic may be an act of genius— for instance, the apperception of the common characteristic between the movement of the planets and the fall of an apple.

lectual discipline among them. The new political attitude of the "clerks" seems to me to be here the result of a serious modification of their state of mind.

This attitude also seems to me to result from the decline of the study of classical literature in the formation of their minds. The humanities, as the word implies, have always taught the cult of humanity in its universal aspect, at least since the time of the Portico.[1] The decline of Graeco-Roman culture in Barrès and his literary generation, in comparison with that of Taine, Renan, Hugo, Michelet, even Anatole France and Bourget, is undeniable. Still less will it be denied that this decline is considerably more noticeable in Barrès's successors. However, this decline does not prevent these writers from extolling classical studies, but they do not do this with the idea of reviving the cult for what is human in its universal aspect, but on the contrary to strengthen the "French" mind, or at least the "Latin" mind, in the grasp of its own roots, in consciousness of itself as distinct from other minds. Notice that this decline of classical culture in the French writers coincides with the discovery of the great German realists, Hegel and especially Nietzsche, whose genius had the more effect on

[1] So much so that the true champions of "sacred egoism" definitely condemn them. Bismarck, Wilhelm II, Naumann, Houston Chamberlain, all argue against classical teaching.

these Frenchmen because their lack of classical discipline deprived them of the one real barrier which can be opposed to that genius.[1]

Among the causes of this new attitude among men of letters I must point to their thirst for sensations, their need to experience things, which in recent times have grown stronger and have caused them to adopt a political attitude which gave them emotions and sensations. Belphegor is not the only star in the literary heavens. A French writer, who was taken seriously as a thinker as early as 1890, was reproached for having joined a party whose inconsistency will long be an amazement to History; and he replied, "I followed Boulangism, as a man follows a fanfare of trumpets." The same thinker gives us to understand that his chief motive in "seeking contact with national minds" was to "throw more fuel under his sensibility, which was beginning to run down."[2] I do not think I am mistaken when I say that numbers of our moralists who sneer at pacific civilization and extol a war-

[1] Remember that Nietzsche only truly esteems the thought of the ancients up to Socrates, i.e. up to the time when it begins to teach the universal.

[2] This same Barrès is quoted as having said to a "Dreyfusist" in 1898: "Why do you talk of justice and humanity to me! What do I care for? A few pictures in Europe and a few cemeteries!" Another of our great political realists confessed one day to his fundamental necessity to "enjoy." Socrates long ago told Protagoras that the basis of his doctrine was a thirst for sensation.

like life, do so because the former seems a dull sort of a life to them and the latter an opportunity for sensations.[1] You will recollect the remark of a young thinker, quoted by Agathon in 1913: "Why not a war? It will be amusing." I shall be told that this is the mere extravagant saying of a young man. But what of this remark from a man of fifty, and what is more, a scientist (R. Quinton), who saw the tragedy of 1914 coming, and exclaimed: "We shall picnic on the grass!"? This scientist was certainly a good soldier, but no more so than Fresnel and Lamarck, of whom I dare to say that they may have approved of war, but not because it satisfied their taste for the picturesque. All who frequented the author of *Reflexions sur la Violence* know that one of the greatest attractions of any idea for him was that it was "amusing" and likely to exasperate so-called reasonable people. There are many thinkers of the past fifty years whose "philosophy" has one fundamental motive— the pleasure of throwing off irritating paradoxes; while they are only too happy if their rockets fall like swords and satisfy that need for cruelty which

[1] It seems to me difficult to deny that pacifism, humanitarianism, and altruism are *boring*. No doubt, art, science, and philosophy offer sufficient opportunities for "amusement" without one asking of it doctrines which set the world on fire. But that is the view of a man who is not wildly eager for sensation.

174

they profess as the sign of noble minds. This prodigious decline of morality, this sort of (very Germanic) intellectual sadism, is usually and quite openly accompanied by a huge contempt for the true "clerk," whose joy comes from the exercise of thought and who disdains sensation, particularly the sensations of action. Here again the new political cult of the men of letters is the result of a modification in the most intimate part of their mind, the very same modification we have been discussing, i.e. a decline of intellectual discipline, which does not mean a decline in intelligence.[1]

On their own showing, many modern "clerks" have adopted these realist doctrines because they want to have done with the moral disarray into which they are thrown by the spectacle of philosophies, "none of which bring certainty," and which all collapse upon each other as they cry to heaven their contradictory absolutes. There again the "clerk's" political attitude is the result of a great decline in his intellectual discipline, whether we consider that this decline is shown by his belief that any philosophy can bring certainty, or whether we

---

[1] The realists are not the only people to-day who find opportunities for sensation in their political attitudes. It is certain that the humanitarianism of Victor Hugo and Michelet is far from having the pure intellectual resonance it had in Spinoza and Malebranche. (See above, my distinction between humanitarianism and humanism.)

175

think that it lies in his inability to stand upright on the ruins of the schools, devoting himself to reason, which is above all the schools, and is their judge.

I shall also admit as one other cause of realism in the modern "clerks" the irritation produced in them by the teaching of some of their predecessors —I mean certain masters of the year 1848, with their visionary idealism, their belief that justice and love were suddenly about to become the essence of the soul of nations, an irritation greatly increased by seeing the dreadful contrast between these idyllic prophecies and the events which followed them. Nevertheless, the point to remember is that the modern "clerks" replied to these errors by hurling anathemas at every sort of idealism, whether visionary or not, thereby showing incapacity to distinguish between species, inability to rise above passion to judgment. And this is but one other aspect of their loss of the good manners of the mind.

Let me recapitulate the causes for this change in the "clerks": The imposition of political interests on all men without any exception; the growth of consistency in matters apt to feed realist passions; the desire and the possibility for men of letters to play a political part; the need in the interests of their own fame for them to play the game of a class which is daily becoming more anxious; the increasing tendency of the "clerks" to become bourgeois and to take on the vanities of that class; the perfecting of their Romanticism; the decline of their knowledge of antiquity and of their intellectual discipline. It will be seen that these causes arise from certain phenomena which are most profoundly and generally characteristic of the present age. The political realism of the "clerks," far from being a superficial fact due to the caprice of an order of men, seems to me bound up with the very essence of the modern world.

IV — SUMMARY — PREDICTIONS

4.

To SUM UP: If I look at contemporary humanity from the point of view of its moral state as revealed by its political life, I see (*a*) A mass in whom realist passions in its two chief forms—class passion, national passion—has attained a degree of consciousness and organization hitherto unknown; (*b*) A body of men who used to be in opposition to the realism of the masses, but who now, not only do not oppose it, but adopt it, proclaim its grandeur and morality; in short, a humanity which has abandoned itself to realism with a unanimity, an absence of reserve, a sanctification of its passion unexampled in history.

This remark may be put in another form. Imagine an observer of the twelfth century taking a bird's-eye view of the Europe of his time. He would see men groping in the obscurity of their minds and striving to form themselves into nations (to mention only the most striking aspect of the realist will); he would see them beginning to succeed; he would see groups of men attaining consistency, determined to seize a portion of the earth and tending to feel conscious of themselves as distinct from the groups surrounding them. But at the same time he would see a whole class of men, regarded with the greatest reverence, laboring to thwart this movement. He would see men of learning, artists and philosophers, displaying to the world a spirit which cared nothing for nations, using a universal language among themselves. He would see those who gave Europe its moral values preaching the cult of the human, or at least of the Christian, and not of the national, he would see them striving to found, in opposition to the nations, a great universal empire on spiritual foundations. And so he might say to himself: "Which of these two currents will triumph? Will humanity be national or spiritual? Will it depend on the will of the laymen or of the "clerks"? And for long ages the realist cause will not be completely victorious; the spiritual body will remain faithful to itself long enough to our observer to be uncertain of the result. To-day the game is over. Humanity is national. The layman has won. But his triumph has gone beyond anything he could have expected. The "clerk" is not only conquered, he is assimilated. The man of science, the artist, the philosopher are attached to their nations as much as the day-laborer and the merchant. Those who make the world's values, make them for a nation; the Ministers of Jesus defend the national. All humanity including the "clerks," have become laymen. All Europe, including Erasmus, has followed Luther.

I said above that the humanity of the past, more precisely the humanity of Europe in the Middle Ages, with the values imposed upon it by the "clerks," acted ill but honored the good. It may be said that modern Europe with teachers who inform it that its realist instincts are beautiful, acts ill and honors what is ill. Modern Europe is like the brigand in one of Tolstoi's stories, who made his confession to a hermit, and the hermit said in amazement: "Others were at least ashamed of being brigands; but what is to be done with this man, who is proud of it?"

Indeed, if we ask ourselves what will happen to a humanity where every group is striving more eagerly than ever to feel conscious of its own particular interests, and makes its moralists tell it that it is sublime to the extent that it knows no law but this interest—a child can give the answer. This humanity is heading for the greatest and most perfect war ever seen in the world, whether it is a war of nations, or a war of classes. A race of which one group exalts one of its masters (Barrès) to the skies because he teaches: "We must defend the essential part of ourselves as sectarians," while a neighboring group acclaims a leader because, when he attacks a defenseless small nation, he says, "Necessity knows no law"—such a race is ripe for the zoölogical wars Renan talks about, which, he said, would be like the life and death wars which occur among rodents and among the carnivora. As regards the nation, think of Italy; as regards class, think of Russia; and you will see the hitherto unknown point of perfection attained by the spirit of hatred against what is "different" among a group of men, consciously realist and at last liberated from all non-practical morality. And my predictions are not rendered less probable by the fact that these two nations are hailed as models throughout the world by those who desire either the grandeur of their nation or the triumph of their class.

These dark predictions do not seem to me to need as much modification as some people think, on account of certain actions resolutely directed against war, such as the setting up of a supernational institution and the agreements recently made by the rival nations. Imposed upon the nations by their Ministers rather than desired by them, dictated solely by interest (the fear of war and its ravages) and not at all by a change in public morality, these new institutions may perhaps be opposed to war but leave intact the *spirit of war,* and nothing leads us to suppose that a nation which only respects a contract for practical reasons, will not break it as soon as breaking it appears more profitable. Peace, if it ever exists, will not be based on the fear of war but on the love of peace. It will not be the abstaining from an act, but the coming of a state of mind.[1] In this sense the most insignificant writer

[1] "Peace is not the absence of war, but a virtue born from strength of soul." (Spinoza.)

can serve peace where the most powerful tribunals can do nothing. And moreover these tribunals leave untouched the economic war between the nations and the class wars.

Peace, it must be repeated after so many others have said this, is only possible if men cease to place their happiness in the possession of things "which cannot be shared," and if they raise themselves to a point where they adopt an abstract principle superior to their egotisms. In other words, it can only be obtained by a betterment of human morality. But, as I have pointed out above, not only do men to-day steel themselves entirely against this, but the very first condition of peace, which is to recognize the necessity for this progress of the soul, is seriously menaced. A school arose in the nineteenth century which told men to expect peace from enlightened self-interest, from the belief that a war, even when victorious, is disastrous, especially to economic transformations, to "the evolution of production," in a phrase, to factors totally foreign to their moral improvement, from which, these thinkers say, it would be frivolous to expect anything. So that humanity, even if it had any desire for peace, is exhorted to neglect the one effort which might procure it, an effort it is delighted not to make. The cause of peace, which is always surrounded with adverse factors, in our days has one more against it—the pacifism which pretends to be scientific.[1]

I can point to other sorts of pacifism, whose chief result I dare to say is to weaken the cause of peace, at least among serious-minded persons:—

(*a*) First, there is the pacifism I shall call "vulgar," meaning thereby the pacifism which does nothing but denounce "the man who kills," and sneer at the prejudices of patriotism. When I see certain teachers, even if they are Montaigne, Voltaire, and Anatole France, whose whole case against war consists in saying that highwaymen are no more criminal than leaders of armies, and in laughing at people who kill each other because one party is dressed in yellow and the other in blue, I feel inclined to desert a cause whose champions oversimplify things to this extent, and I begin to feel some sympathy for the impulses of profound humanity which created the nations and which are thereby so grossly insulted.[2]

[1] Here is an example: "Universal peace will come about one day, not because men will become better (one cannot hope for that) but because a new order of things, new science, new economic needs, will impose a state of peace on them, just as the very conditions of their existence formerly placed and maintained them in a state of war." (Anatole France, *Sur la Pierre blanche.*) Note the refusal, mentioned above, to believe in any possible betterment of the human soul.

[2] This observation applied to nearly all anti-militarist literature up to our own times. We have to come to Renan and Renouvier (at least among writers not of the Church) to find authors who speak of war and national passions with the seriousness and respect due to such dramas.

(*b*) *Mystic pacifism*, by which I mean the pacifism which is solely animated by a blind hatred of war and refuses to inquire whether a war is just or not, whether those fighting are the attackers or the defenders, whether they wanted war or only submit to it. This pacifism is essentially the pacifism of the people (and that of all the so-called pacifist newspapers) and was strikingly embodied in 1914 by a French writer who, having to judge between two fighting nations one of which had attacked the other contrary to all its pledges while the other was only defending itself, could do nothing but intone "I have a horror of war" and condemned them both equally. It is impossible to exaggerate the consequences of this behavior, which showed mankind that mystic pacifism, just like mystic militarism, may entirely obliterate the feeling of justice in those who are smitten with it.

I think I see another motive in the French writers who in 1914 adopted the attitude of M. Romain Rolland—the fear that they would fall into national partiality if they admitted that their nation was in the right. It may be asserted that these writers would have warmly taken up the cause of France, if France had not been their own country. Whereas Barrès said, "I always maintain my country is right even if it is in the wrong," these strange friends of justice are not unwilling to say: "I always maintain my country is in the wrong, even if

it is right." There again we see that the frenzy of
impartiality, like any other frenzy, leads to injustice.

I have also a word to say about the severities of
these "justiciaries" towards France's attitude immediately after her victory, towards her desire to
force the enemy to make good the damage done to
her, and to seize on pledges if he refused. The motive which here animated these moralists without
their perceiving it, seems to me very remarkable; it
was the thought that the just person must inevitably
be weak and suffer, that he must be a victim. If
the just man becomes strong and comes to possess
the means of enforcing justice towards himself,
then he ceases to be just to these thinkers. If
Socrates and Jesus make their persecutors disgorge,
then they cease to embody justice; one step more
and the persecutors, having become victims, would
embody right. In this the cult of justice is replaced
by the cult of misfortune, a Christian Romanticism
which is somewhat unexpected in a man like
Anatole France. No doubt the events of 1918 up-
set all the habits of the advocates of right. Out-
raged right became the stronger, the assailed toga
triumphed over the sword, the Curiatii were victorious. Perhaps some coolness of mind was needed
to recognize that right remained right, even when
thus invested with force. The French pacifists
failed to remain cool. In short, their attitude in

the past ten years has been inspired by sentiment alone, and nothing could show better the degree of weakness to which intellectual discipline has now fallen among our "princes of the mind." [1]

(c) *Pacifism claiming to be patriotic,* by which I mean the pacifism which claims to exalt humanitarianism, to preach the abatement of the militarist spirit and of national passion, and yet not to harm the interests of the nation nor to compromise its power of resistance to foreign nations. This attitude—which is that of all Parliamentary pacifists—is the more antipathetic to upright minds in that it is inevitably accompanied by the assertion (which is also nearly always contrary to the truth) that the nation is not in the least threatened and that the malevolence of neighboring nations is a pure invention of people who want war. But that is merely an aspect of a very general fact, which is of supreme importance to the matter under discussion.

By this I mean the "clerk's" determination to put

---

[1] I am not to say whether the claims of France after her victory might have been *impolitic,* for the thinkers I am discussing here only speak of what they consider their *immorality.* Notice that the pacifism of the Church, at least among the great teachers, is not at all inspired by sentimental considerations, but by pure moral education. "What do we condemn in war?" says Saint Augustine. "Is it the fact that they kill men who have all one day to die? Only cowards, not religious men, would bring this accusation against war. What we condemn in war is the desire to do harm, an implacable soul, the fury of reprisals, the passion for dominion." (This is taken up by Thomas Aquinas in the *Summum,* 2, 2, xl, art. 1.)

forth his principles as valid in the practical order of things, as reconcilable with the safeguarding of the sword's conquests. This determination, which has affected the Church for twenty centuries and almost all the idealists (give me the names of those since Jesus who have declared themselves incompetent in the practical order of things), is the source of all the "clerk's failures." It may be said that the "clerk's" defeat begins from the very moment when he claims to be practical. As soon as the "clerk" claims that he does not disregard the interests of the nation or of the established classes, he is inevitably beaten, for the very good reason that it is impossible to preach the spiritual and the universal without undermining the institutions whose foundations are the possession of the material and the desire to feel distinct from others. A true "clerk" (Renan) says excellently: "The mother-country is a worldly thing; the man who wants to play the angel will always be a bad patriot." Thus we see that the "clerk" who claims to secure the works of the world has a choice between two consequences. Either he secures them and transgresses all his principles, which is the case with the Church supporting the nation and property; or he maintains his principles and causes the ruin of the institutions he claimed he was supporting, which is the case with the humanitarian who claims to safeguard what is national. In the first case the "clerk"

is despised by the just man, who denounces him as
cunning and strikes him out of the rank of "clerk";
and in the second case he collapses under the hoot-
ing of the nations who call him inefficient, while he
provokes a violent and loudly acclaimed reaction on
the part of the realist, which is what is now happening in Italy. From all this it follows that the
"clerk" is only strong if he is clearly conscious of
his essential qualities and his true function, and
shows mankind that he is clearly conscious of them.
In other words he declares to them that his kingdom is not of this world, that *the grandeur of his
teaching lies precisely in this absence of practical
value, and that the right morality for the prosperity
of the kingdoms which are of this world, is not his,
but Caesar's.* When he takes up this position, the
"clerk" is crucified, but he is respected, and his
words haunt the memory of mankind.[1] The need
to remind the modern "clerks" of these truths (for
every one of them is angry at being called Utopian)
is one of the most suggestive observations in connection with our subject. It shows that the desire

[1] I consider that "My kingdom is not of this world" may be
said by all whose activity is not directed to practical ends:
The artist, the metaphysician, the scientist *insofar as he finds
satisfaction in the practice of science and not in its results.*
Many will tell me that they and not the Christians are the
true "clerks," for the Christian accepts the ideas of justice
and charity only for the sake of his salvation. No one will
deny, however, that men, even Christians, exist, who accept
this idea with no practical end in view.

to be practical has become general, that the claim to be so has now become necessary in order to obtain an audience, and that the very notion of "clerkdom" has become obscured even in those who still tend to exercise that function.

It will be seen that I entirely dissociate myself from those who want the "clerk" to govern the world, and who wish with Renan for the "reign of the philosophers"; for it seems to me that human affairs can only adopt the religions of the true "clerk" under penalty of becoming divine, i.e. of perishing as human. This has been clearly seen by all lovers of the divine who did not desire the destruction of what is human. This is marvelously expressed by one of them when he makes Jesus say so profoundly to His disciple: "My son, I must not give you a clear idea of your substance . . . for if you saw clearly what you are, you could no longer remain so closely united to your body. You would no longer watch over the preservation of your life."[1] But though I think it a bad thing that the "clerk's" religion should possess the lay world, I think it still more to be dreaded that it should not be preached to the layman at all, and that he should thus be allowed to yield to his practical passions without the least shame or the least, even hypocritical, desire to raise himself however slightly above them. "There are a few just men who pre-

[1] Malebranche, *Méditations chrétiennes* (ix, 19).

192

vent me from sleeping"——that was what the realist
said of the teachers of old. Nietzsche, Barrès, and
Sorel do not prevent any realist from sleeping; on
the contrary. This is the novelty I want to point
out, which to me seems so serious. It seems to me
serious that a humanity, which is more than ever
obsessed by the passions of the world, should receive
from its spiritual leaders the command: "Remain
faithful to the earth."

Is this adoption of "integral realism" by the human species permanent, or merely temporary?
Are we, as some people think, witnessing the beginning of a new Middle Ages (and one far more
barbarous than the former, for though it practiced
realism, it did not extol realism), from which, however, will arise a new Renaissance, a new return to
the religion of distinterestedness? The elements we
have discovered as forming the new realism scarcely
allow us to hope so. It is hard to imagine the nations sincerely striving not to feel conscious of
themselves as distinct from others, or, if they do so,
having any other motive than that of concentrat-
ing inter-human hatred into that of class. It is
hard to imagine the clergy regaining a real moral
sway over the faithful and being able (supposing
they desired to do so) to tell them with impunity
unpleasant truths. It is hard to imagine a body of
men of letters (for corporative action becomes
more and more important) attempting to with-

stand the bourgeois classes instead of flattering them. It is still harder to imagine them turning against the tide of their intellectual decadence and ceasing to think that they display a lofty culture when they sneer at rational morality and fall on their knees before history. Nevertheless one thinks of a humanity of the future, weary of its "sacred egotisms" and the slaughterings to which they inevitably lead, coming as humanity came two thousand years ago, to the acceptance of a good situated beyond itself, accepting it even more ardently than before, with the knowledge of all the tears and blood that have been shed through departing from that doctrine. Once more Vauvenargue's admirable saying would be verified. "The passions have taught men reason." But such a thing only seems to me possible after a long lapse of time, when war has caused far more woes than have yet been endured. Men will not revise their values for wars which only last fifty months and only kill a couple of million men in each nation. One may even doubt whether war will ever become so terrible as to discourage those who love it, the more so since they are not always the men who have to fight.

When I set this limit to my pessimistic outlook and admit that such a Renaissance is possible, I mean no more than that it is just possible. I cannot agree with those who say it is certain, either because it happened once before, or because "civilization is due to the human race." Civilization as I understand it here—moral supremacy conferred on the cult of the spiritual and on the feeling of the universal—appears to me as a lucky accident in man's development. It blossomed three thousand years ago under a set of circumstances whose contingent character was perfectly perceived by the historian who called it "the Greek miracle." It does not appear to me in the least to be a thing due to the human race by virtue of the data of its nature. It seems to me so little such a thing that I observe large portions of the species (the Asiatic world in antiquity, the Germanic world in modern times) who showed themselves incapable of it and quite likely to remain so. And this means that if humanity loses this jewel, there is not much chance of finding it again. On the contrary there is every chance that humanity will not find it again, just as a man who should find a precious stone in the sea and then drop it back in the water would have little chance of ever seeing it again. Nothing seems to me more doubtful than Aristotle's remark that it is probable the arts and philosophy have several times been discovered and several times lost. The other position which maintains that civilization, despite partial eclipses, is something which humanity cannot lose, seems to me quite worthless except as an act of faith—though it is valuable as a means of preserving the good we wish to keep. I should not think it a serious objection to what I have said if some one should point out that civilization, lost once with the fall of the ancient world, nevertheless had its Renaissance. Every one knows that the Graeco-Roman form of mind was far from being wholly extinguished during the Middle Ages and that the sixteenth century only brought to life what was not dead; to which I add that even if that form of mind had been "reborn" *ex nihilo,* the fact that this is the only instance would make it insufficient to reassure me, although the fact that it had occurred would disturb me.

Let me point out in this respect that insufficient attention is perhaps paid to the fact that there are always only a very tiny number of instances in history on which are built up a "law," which claims to be valid for the whole past and future evolution of humanity. Vico says that history is a series of alternations between periods of progress and periods of retrogression; and he gives *two* examples. Saint-Simon says history is a series of oscillations between organic epochs and critical epochs; and he gives *two* examples. Marx says history is a series of economic systems, each of which casts out its predecessor by means of violence; and he gives *one* example. I shall be told that these examples could not be more numerous, owing to the fact that history, at least known history, is so short. The truth, implied by this very reply, is that history has lasted too short a time for us to be able to deduce laws from it to enable us to infer the future from the past. Those who do so are like a mathematician who should decide the nature of a curve from the form he finds it has at its very beginning. True, a somewhat uncommon turn of mind is required to confess that human history, after several thousands of years, is only beginning. I cannot sufficiently admire the rare mental value displayed by La Bruyère (in my opinion) when he wrote the following lines in a century which was strongly inclined to think it was the topmost summit of human development: "If the world lasts only a hundred million years, it will still be in all its freshness and only beginning; we ourselves are almost contemporary with the first men and the patriarchs, and who, in those far-off ages, will be able to avoid confusing us with them? But if we judge of the future from the past, what new things are we ignorant of in the arts, in the sciences, in Nature, and, I dare say, in history? What discoveries will be made! What different revolutions will occur in our Empires all over the world! How ignorant we are! And how slight is an experience of six or seven thousand years!"

I shall go further and say that even if an examination of the past could lead to any valid prediction concerning man's future, that prediction would be the contrary of reassuring. People forget that Hellenic rationalism only really enlightened the world during seven hundred years, that it was then hidden (this *a minima* verdict will be granted me) for twelve centuries, and has begun to shine again for barely four centuries; so that *the longest period of consecutive time in human history on which we can found inductions is, upon the whole, a period of intellectual and moral darkness.* Looking at history, we may say in a more synthetic manner that, with the exception of two or three very short, luminous epochs whose light, like that of certain stars, lightens the world long after they are extinct, humanity lives generally in darkness; while literatures live generally in a state of decadence and the organism in disorder. And the disturbing thing is that humanity does not seem to mind these long periods of cave-dwelling.

To come back to the realism of my contemporaries and their contempt for a distinterested existence, I must add that my mind is sometimes haunted by a dreadful question. I wonder whether humanity, by adopting this system to-day, has not discovered its true law of existence and adopted the true scale of values demanded by its essence? The religion of the spiritual, I said just now, seems to me a lucky accident in man's history. I shall go further, and say it seems to me a paradox. The obvious law of human substance is the conquest of things and the exaltation of the impulses which secure this conquest. Only through an amazing abuse were a handful of men at desks able to succeed in making humanity believe that the supreme values are the good things of the spirit. To-day humanity has awakened from this dream, knows its true nature and its real desires, and utters its warcry against those who for centuries have robbed it of itself. Instead of waxing indignant at the ruin of their domination, would it not be more reasonable for these usurpers (if there are any left) to wonder that it lasted so long? Orpheus could not aspire to charm the wild beasts with his music until the end of time. However, one could have hoped that Orpheus himself would not become a wild beast.

It is scarcely necessary to say my remarks on realist desires and their violent perfecting do not blind me to the immense growth of gentleness, justice, and love written to-day in our customs and laws, which would certainly have amazed our most optimistic ancestors. There is an immense improvement in the relations between man and man within the groups which fight each other—especially within the nation where security is the rule and injustice is a scandal. But to keep more closely to our subject, perhaps we do not sufficiently realize the incredible degree of civilization implied by the good treatment of prisoners, and the care of enemy wounded in wars between nations, and by the institution of public and private charity in the relations between the classes. The denial of progress, the assertion that barbarity of heart has never been worse, are natural themes for poets and those who are discontented, and perhaps they are even necessary to progress. But the historian, whether he looks at national or class warfare, is amazed at the transformation of a species which only four centuries ago roasted prisoners of war in baker's ovens, and, only two centuries ago forbade the workers to establish a pension fund for their aged members. Nevertheless I must point out that these improvements cannot be credited to the present age. They are the results of the teaching of the eighteenth century, against which the "masters of modern thought" are in complete revolt. The establishment of war ambulances, the wide development of State charities are the work of the Second Empire, are connected with the "humanitarian clichés" of Victor Hugo and Michelet, which are immeasurably despised by the moralists of the past half century. They exist to some extent *despite of* these moralists, not one of whom has conducted a truly humane campaign, while the chief of them— Nietzsche, Barrès, Sorel—would blush to be able to say like Voltaire: "I have done a little good, 'tis my best work." I must add that these good works are now merely customs, i.e. actions performed from habit, without the will taking any part in them, without the mind reflecting on their meaning. And if the mind of our realists ever came to think of them, I think there is every possibility that it might prohibit them. I can well imagine a future war when a nation would decide not to look after the enemy wounded, a strike where the bourgeoisie would make up its mind not to support hospitals for the benefit of a class which was ruining it and anxious to destroy it. I can imagine both priding themselves on getting free from a "stupid humanitarianism," and finding disciples of Nietzsche and Sorel to praise them for it. The attitude of the Italian Fascists and the Russian Bolshevists towards their enemies is not calculated to give me the lie here. The modern world still displays certain failures in pure practicality, a few stains of idealism from which it might well cleanse itself.

I said above that the logical end of the "integral realism" professed by humanity to-day is the organized slaughter of nations or classes. It is possible to conceive of a third, which would be their reconciliation. The thing to possess would be the whole earth, and they would finally come to realize that the only way to exploit it properly is by union, while the desire to set themselves up as distinct from others would be transferred from the nation to the species, arrogantly drawn up against everything which is not itself. And, as a matter of fact, such a movement does exist. Above classes and nations there does exist a desire of the species to become the

master of things, and, when a human being flies
from one end of the world to the other in a few
hours, the whole human race quivers with pride
and adores itself as distinct from all the rest of
creation. At bottom, this imperialism of the species
is preached by all the great directors of the modern
conscience. It is Man, and not the nation or the
class, whom Nietzsche, Sorel, Bergson extol in his
genius for making himself master of the world. It
is humanity, and not any one section of it, whom
Auguste Comte exhorts to plunge into consciousness of itself and to make itself the object of its
adoration. Sometimes one may feel that such an
impulse will grow ever stronger, and that in this
way inter-human wars will come to an end. In
this way humanity would attain "universal fraternity." But, far from being the abolition of the
national spirit with its appetites and its arrogance,
this would simply be its supreme form, the nation
being called Man and the enemy God. Thereafter,
humanity would be unified in one immense army,
one immense factory, would be aware only of hero-
isms, disciplines, inventions, would denounce all
free and distinterested activity, would long cease to
situate the good outside the real world, would have
no God but itself and its desires, and would achieve
great things; by which I mean that it would attain
to a really grandiose control over the matter surrounding it, to a really joyous consciousness of its

power and its grandeur. And History will smile to think that this is the species for which Socrates and Jesus Christ died.

1924-1927.

NOTES

NOTE A

(Page 3)

That political passions affect a large number of men they never before affected . . .

It is every difficult to know to what extent crowds are moved by the political events of their time (of course, I am leaving on one side all truly popular movements). Crowds do not write their memoirs, and those who write memoirs scarcely ever speak of the crowds. However, I do not think my proposition will be seriously disputed. To limit ourselves to France and the two examples I quoted —suppose we had another upheaval like the Religious Wars, I do not think we should see the immense majority of country districts possessed by no other passion than a hatred for soldiers, whatever party they belonged to.[1] Nor should we see cultivated bourgeois who keep diaries giving a couple of lines to such events as Luther's preaching, along

[1] See Babeau, *Le village sous l'ancien régime*, iv, iii; L. Gregoire, *La Ligue en Bretagne*, chap. vi; Roupnel, *La Ville et la Campagne au xvii siècle*, i, 1. "The peasants," says M. Roumier, "were only really converted where it was to their interests to be so, and especially where the local landlords put their influence at the service of the new religion, and where the Catholic clergy had completely deserted the parishes. We must be careful not to consider as Protestants all the 'rustics' who took part in pillaging the abbeys and castles during the civil war" (*La Royaume de Catherine de Médicis*, tome ii, page 294). M. Romier quotes the remark of a contemporary: "The whole of the Low Countries scarcely knows what this new doctrine is."

with the thousand little facts they relate.[1] Nor do
I think that a month after an event like the taking
of the Bastille we should find a foreigner on his
travels in France, writing: "13th August, 1789.
Before I leave Clermont I must remark that I have
dined or supped five times at the table d'hôte with
some twenty to thirty merchants and tradesmen,
officers, etc.; and it is not easy for me to express the
insignificance—the inanity of the conversation.
Scarcely any politics, at a moment when every
bosom ought to beat with none but political sensations." (Arthur Young.) [2]

The attitude of populations towards wars between States long seems to have been that described
by Voltaire in the following lines: "It is indeed a
deplorable evil that this multitude of soldiers should

[1] "Le livre de raison de M. Nicolas Versoris" (*Mémoires de
la Société de l'Histoire de Paris*, tome xii). The author,
avocat au Parlement de Paris, similarly gives two lines to
events like the Connétable de Bourbon's treachery, and the
signing of the treaty of Madrid. The same attitude exists in
the *Journal d'un Bourgeois de Paris*, 1515-1536; the public
misfortunes sketched by the author leave him completely indifferent. He makes no comment on the disaster of Pavia.
Apropos the treaty of Madrid, "It is to be noted," writes a
contemporary, "that there were no bonfires or rejoicings when
the news of the peace was published, because no one understood anything about it." (Lavisse, *Histoire de France*, v.
49.) Contemporaries mention the indifference of the people
of Paris to the Peace of Westphalia, the battle of Rossbach,
even the battles of Valmy and Navarino. "The affair at
Valmy made very little stir at first." (Kellerman.)

[2] Michelet relates that in his youth he questioned an old
man on the impressions left upon him by 1793, and the only
answer he got was: "It was the bad paper year."

208

always be kept up by all Princes. But, as we have pointed out, this evil produces a good. The peoples take no part in the wars carried on by their masters; the citizens of besieged towns often pass from the power of one to another without having cost the life of a single inhabitant; they are simply the prize of the King who possesses most soldiers, cannons and money." (*Essai sur les Moeurs,* towards the end.) Again, in 1870, a Prussian servant girl said to a French prisoner employed on the farm where she was working: "When the war is over I will marry you. Don't be surprised at what I say, patriotism doesn't mean much to us, you know." I imagine that in 1914, many servant girls, Prussian or otherwise, felt in their hearts and put into practice, this absence of patriotism; but I dare to assert that very few would have formulated it, even to themselves. The really new fact to-day is not perhaps that the peoples feel political passions, but that they claim the right to feel them. This claim is sufficient to make them act and therefore furnishes a magnificent opportunity for their leaders to exploit them.

NOTE B

(Page 20)

Louis XIV annexing Alsace and not for one moment thinking of forbidding the German language . . .

It was not until 1768 that the Monarchy thought of setting up schools in Alsace, "where French is to be taught." Vidal de la Blanche, who relates this (*La France de l'Est*, 1, vi) adds: "This indifference (to the language question) must not shock us too much. Let us rather learn a lesson from it. It raises us above the narrowly jealous conceptions which since then have set nation against nation, under this language pretext. It takes us into an age when another spirit presided over human relations. There was then no language question. Fortunate eighteenth century, when war bred no lasting hatred, when the poison of national animosities was not inoculated and fostered by all the means now at the disposal of the State, including the schools." The eminent historian forgets that the State has these means at its disposal, *with the consent of the peoples.* The peoples, or at least the cultivated classes among them, at the bidding of their men of letters, during the past century have set themselves up arrogantly against one another in their languages and cultures, even though they one day come face to face with the unexpected results of this attitude, as is happening to-day to France in its difficulties with Alsace.

NOTE C

(Page 24)

The Union of capitalism, anti-semiteism, anti-democracy with nationalism.

I am under no illusion concerning the solidity of certain among these unions. Although the conservative passions fully comprehend their immense interest in identifying themselves with national passion and thereby benefiting by its popularity, although one may even admit that they have been caught in their own net and have become sincere in this feeling, yet it is none the less true that conservatism (chiefly capitalism) is essentially something entirely different from patriotism, and that this difference, whose manifestations in the course of history have been innumerable (how many times have the bourgeoisie treated with foreigners when they thought it was to their interests!) may once again display itself. It is easy to imagine that the French bourgeoisie would turn against France if they thought their patrimony was being too seriously threatened by the legislation of the Republic. This may already be seen in the case of families who, in recent years, have exported their capital abroad. I may say the same thing of monarchist passion. It is easy to imagine that certain followers of that passion might one day decide to work against a nation which decisively and finally rejects the system they propose. I think I observe this when I see monarchist writers publishing that "from the Spree to the Mekong, the whole world knows that France is in a state of weakness bordering upon disintegration." However, such things are still exceptional, and those who are responsible for them would refuse to admit—perhaps sincerely —that they meant to harm their nation.

Moreover, the bourgeoisie have another interest in keeping up nationalism and the fear of war. These feelings create a sort of permanent military spirit in a nation. More precisely, they create in the people a disposition to accept the existing hierarchy, to obey orders, to recognize superiors, i.e. the very things required of them by those who wish them to continue in a state of service. The confused perception of this truth inspires the bourgeoisie with that curious ill-humor they display towards every attempt at international agreement, in whatever form this may be presented by the governments. This ill-humor (they declare) arises from the fact that they consider it simple-minded and imprudent to believe in the extinction of national hatreds. At bottom, it arises from the fact that *they do not want this extinction to occur.* They know that the maintenance of these hatreds will cost the lives of their children, but they do not hesitate to make the sacrifice, if by doing so they retain possession of their property [1] and their power

---

[1] Admire the profundity of Machiavelli, when he advises his Prince: "Above everything, avoid taking your subjects' property; *for men will more easily forget the deaths of their fathers than the loss of their patrimony.*"

over their servants. Here is a grandeur of egotism
which is perhaps insufficiently appreciated.

NOTE D
(Page 38)

*On the attitude of the modern Catholics towards
Catholicism when it is in opposition to their nationalism.*

A good example is the attitude of the German
Catholics in the past twenty years. It has been described with all desirable detail by M. Edmond
Bloud in his great study: *Le nouveau Centre et le
catholicisme.*[1] It will be seen that it strangely
resembles the attitude of many a non-German
Catholic.

The "Centre" began by declaring itself "a political party which has assumed as its duty the representation of the interests of the whole nation in all
domains of public life, in accordance with the principles of Christian doctrine. (*Katholische Weltan-
schauung:* Catholic conception of the world.)
Soon they announced political action founded on
"a Christian basis" (christliche Basis), the spirit of
which is thus defined by one of its apostles (Doctor
Brauweiler, April, 1913): "In the domain of practical action, *concepts are determined by the end in
view.* The formation of political concepts is com-

[1] Inserted in the collection of studies entitled "L'Allemagne
et les Alliés devant la conscience chrétienne." (Bloud et Gay,
1915.)

parable with the formation of juridical concepts. The jurist forms his concepts *with no other consideration than that of what is needed, in relation solely to the required end.* But no one can say that the juridical concept thus formed is a false one. In the same way, one may speak in politics of Christianity or Christian doctrine. In 1914, Doctor Karl Bachem of Cologne, published a pamphlet entitled: *Centre, Catholic Doctrine, Practical Politics,* where he declares that the doctrine of "universal Christianity" is only a political formula intended to render possible the collaboration of Catholics and Protestants, chiefly in Parliament; that from the religious point of view this formula has only a negative meaning, and only means the determination to struggle against materialism, atheism and nihilism; that its positive content is defined by the Prussian Constitution which in paragraphs 14 and 18 lays down that "the Christian religion" is the "foundation of the institutions of the State."

Thus, as M. Edmond Bloud justly remarks, Doctor Bachem makes the Prussian Constitution the Rule of Faith. Put "national interest" in place of "Prussian Constitution" and you will have the state of mind of many a modern French Catholic.

The attitude of the German Catholics seems to me also representative of a certain Catholicism common to-day to other nations, in declarations of this sort:

"The Catholic members of the 'Centre' remain Catholics individually, *but the party, as a party, does not necessarily accept the Catholic conception of the world."*

And again:

"The Pope and the Bishops have authority in matters of religion, but wherever political matters are concerned we shall not allow ourselves to be influenced by the authority of the Pope or by that of the Bishops." (M. Edmond Bloud alludes to a conversation reported in the *Frankfurter Zeitung,* April, 1914, where one of the chief of the "syndicats mixtes" declared that, "The German Catholics have had enough of the Pope.")

What M. Bloud calls the "declericalization of the Centre" is not a thing peculiar to our neighbors, nor is the joy of the great German nationalist organ (the Prussian Annals) when it observes that "the Catholic idea of the State is ceasing to be ultramontane and is becoming nationalist." [1]

The attitude common to German Catholics and to certain Catholics of other nations seems to me well brought out by two protests which M. Bloud quotes.

The first is from Father Weiss:

"There exist," says the eminent theologian, "several kinds of political Catholicism. . . . The worst of all consists in looking upon pure politics,

[1] M. Edmond Bloud quotes this remark of a German nationalist, which might have been made on the French side of the Rhine: "The Catholic world must be nationalized to re-Catholicize it." He adds that in Germany it is common to hear "German Catholicism" spoken of in opposition to Roman Catholicism.

social politics, national politics, not only as something wholly independent of religion, but *as being the standard by which we should determine the degree to which Catholicism or Christianity may be utilized in public life.*"

The other is from Cardinal Kopp (then Bishop of Fulda) in a letter written in 1887:

"Unhappily a gust of madness is blowing over us. Formerly we held to the principle: Faith first, politics afterwards. Now they say: *Politics first!* The Church and the Faith afterwards."

Our Catholics of the *Action Française* have not invented much.

NOTE E

(Page 47)

The "clerk" by adopting political passions, brings them the tremendous influence of his sensibility if he is an artist, of his persuasive power if he is a thinker, and in either case his moral prestige.

This prestige itself is something new in history, at least from my point of view. The results produced in France by the intervention of the "intellectuals" in the Dreyfus affair, and those produced by the manifesto of the German Intellectuals in 1914, not only in their own country but throughout the world, are things to which I find no equivalent in the past. One cannot imagine the Roman Republic feeling that the moral support of Terence and Varro was of value to it during the war with

216

Carthage, or the government of Louis XIV finding that the approbation of Racine and Fermat, gave it additional strength in the war with Holland. This increase of strength which a cause to-day receives from the approbation of the men of thought (or those who are considered such) does great honor to the modern world. It is an homage to the mind hitherto unexampled in humanity.

Naturally, this prestige has a double result. Though the modern "clerk" fortifies a cause by giving it his approbation he can also seriously harm it by refusing his approbation. If in 1915 men like Ostwald and Mach had refused to approve the acts of their nation, they would have seriously harmed it. The "clerk" who to-day condemns the realism of the State to which he belongs does really harm that State.[1] Hence it follows that the State, in the name of its practical interests, to defend which is its function, has a right—perhaps a duty—to punish them. This appears to me to be the true order of things: The "clerk," faithful to his essential duty, denounces the realism of States; whereupon, the States, no less faithful to their duty, made him drink the hemlock. The serious disorganization in the modern world is that the "clerks" do not denounce the realism of States, but on the contrary approve of it; they no longer drink the hemlock.[2]

[1] And therefore it requires much more courage to do so now than in the past.

[2] Nevertheless, Zola, Romain Rolland, and Einstein have drunk the hemlock.

217

Let me point to another disorganization. That is when the State does not punish the "clerk" for denouncing its realism. This occurred in France during the Dreyfus affair. The order of things demanded that the "clerks" should demand abstract justice. as they did; but perhaps it also demanded that the State, weakened in strength by their idealism, should throw them into prison. When the "clerk" performs the layman's task, the result is anarchy; but there is also anarchy when the layman acts and speaks as a "clerk," when those whose duty is to defend the nation display their cult for the abolition of frontiers, universal love, or other spiritual things.[1] When I see philosophers concerning themselves with the safety of the State and Ministers striving to bring about love among mankind, I think of what Dante says: "You turn to religion him who was born to wear the sword, you make a King of one who was born to preach. Thus all your steps are out of the true way." However, this second disorganization of orders has been denounced by others, and it is not my function to combat it.

[1] When they allow themselves to be told, as Louis XVI was told by Turgot: "Sire, your kingdom *is of this world.*" There also exists *"a betrayal of the laymen."*

*Think how willingly the ecclesiastics now accept
military service.*

I think this willingness is worthy of the historian's attention. Obviously, it implies some sincere attachment to their country in those who
display this willingness, although their law is to be
dead to all worldly attachments. Moreover, it appears that in the last war most of the ministers of
Jesus Christ able to bear arms were glad to defend
their country, whatever that country was, and
whatever notion they may have had of the justice
of its cause. Here is a most suggestive fact: Certain
Belgian monastic orders (and others as well, I am
told) established abroad at the declaration of war,
and authorized by the government to remain
abroad, insisted upon returning to the capital to
perform their military duties. True, the behavior
of these monks may be explained, not on grounds
of patriotism, but from the fear that they would
be severely criticized by their fellow-citizens if they
acted otherwise; for the modern "clerks" have
ceased to understand that the sign of an attitude
truly in harmony with their function is that it
should be unpopular with the laymen.

But the most remarkable thing here for the historian, is that the imposition of military service on
ecclesiastics does not appear to arouse any protest
from the Church. Certain Church teachers even

assert (Mgr. Battifol, *L'Eglise et le Droit de la guerre*): "There is no further doubt about the legality of military service." [1] It is also curious to see in the *Dictionnaire apologetique de la foi catholique* (Art. "Paix et Guerre") the strenuous efforts of the author (Father de la Brière) to prove that bearing arms, even by "clerks" in holy orders, is in no sense contrary to Christian law. However, the opinion of these theologians does not seem to be shared, at least publicly, by the higher ecclesiastical authorities; for every "clerk" who bears arms is laid under an interdict, as he was in the past—only the interdict is taken off a few minutes after it has been declared.

The modern laymen (Barrès for example) praise this patriotism of the ecclesiastic and his willingness to fight. The laymen of the past tried to make him ashamed of it, and liked to exhort him to sentiments which they considered more in harmony with his sacred ministry. The warlike ardors of John XII and Julius II were severely condemned by their contemporaries. Apart from Erasmus, the type of the man of letters fully aware of the "clerk's" high function, who was continually saying: "Their tonsure does not warn them that they ought to be free from all the passions of this world and think only of the things of Heaven," the Italian Tizio

---

[1] Mgr. Battifol's writings support my argument so beautifully that I hesitate to quote an author who plays so perfectly into my hands. For example, he spends much time in proving that the spirit of Christianity "has resulted, with contradicting itself, in a doctrine of the morality of war."

wrote: "It is astonishing that the Pontiffs, whose part is to be pacific and independent, should take part in the shedding of Christian blood." The French poet Jean Bouchet shows the weeping Church imploring Julius II to end the war (though it is true that Julius II was fighting France):

> "Your patron is my Lord Saint Peter,
> Who never warred for worldly goods."

In *Le Songe du Verger*, a kind of summary of moral doctrines current in France in the fourteenth century, there is a dialogue between a Knight and a Clerk, when the Clerk claims for his caste the right to make war, and the Knight tells him that "the arms of the 'clerks' are prayers and tears." It is suggestive to see a soldier urging a minister of the spiritual to perform his true function and seeming to think that the performance of this function is necessary to the good order of the world. Here is a feeling for "clerkdom" and its social value which is very seldom to be found among the modern laymen, even the non-military ones—I nearly said, especially the non-military ones.[1]

[1] Here is a passage which, except for its violence, seems to me to express the feelings of most modern laymen on the subject of the patriotic loyalty of the priests: "The clergy of France is ardently patriotic; it serves gallantly under fire; it absolves and glorifies every action of the soldier; it regards the accusation of having deserted military duty as infamous, and does it justice. It is not for me to say whether it is in accord with the Gospels. We are simply Frenchmen and patriots; we can only approve and admire the French patriotic monks and priests. The French priest has no pardon for a German,

NOTE G

(Page 71)

That self-examination to which every spectator is impelled by a representation of human beings which he feels to be true and solely pre-occupied with truth.

Let me quote the following passage concerning the civilizing effects of such representation:—

"This spectacle of man offered to man has considerable moral effects. First, a valuable exercise of the intelligence, an increase of reflection, a widening of the view in every direction, result from the habit thus set up of getting out of oneself and entering into others, to understand their actions, to share in their passions, sympathize with their sufferings, appreciate their motives. This faculty of the artist communicated to the spectator or the listener, this faculty of participation and assimilation, is something set up in opposition to egotism and is a condition of tolerance and benevolence, frequently even of justice. Then, lessons of virtue, frequently not the least effective, are given to the spectator, from the very fact that he is placed in a position to praise or condemn acts or thoughts which are set before him relative to cases where his own interests

the German priest and pastor have no pardon for a Frenchman. Mother-country first! Kill! Kill! In the name of the God of the Christians, we absolve you, we glorify you for killing Christians!" (Urbain Gohier, "La Vieille France," quoted by Grillot de Givry, *Le Christ et la Patrie,* page 12.)

are not involved. He recognizes his own image in the actor of the epic, a man like himself, a voluntary and impassioned agent, whose dangers though perhaps magnified are not foreign to his own experience. Then the essential phenomena which characterize conscious humanity and morality occur in him who thus witnesses himself in the person of another, i.e. distinterested objectivity of himself to himself, generalization of passion, motive and maxim, judgment founded on the universal, self-examination to arrive at what is duty, clear and defined sentiment of the direction of the will.

"But this must not lead us to think that the poet's object is utility or morality. If it were, he would be lacking in the true feeling of art. Teaching, moralizing—this object of the artist is indirect, i.e. does not exist systematically for him. He must only attain it without having sought it, and sometimes he attains it when he seems to have departed from it. What he desires to do, is to touch the feelings, to arouse emotions. But it happens that by doing so he elevates, purifies, moralizes. The poet (I am especially speaking of him) does indeed address himself to every one. That means he can only sing the universal, however curious such an assembly of words may appear. He may indeed sing it under the form of the particular, without which his fictions would be lacking in life, he none the less excludes the pure, incomprehensible, inexplicable individual, shorn of all truth if he does not express a relationship.[1] He generalizes passion, therefore ennobles it and renders it at once the object of observation, reflection and disinterested emotion. The listener, carried away from his own relatively base private preoccupations and transported without hope or fear (at least, too personal and too present hope and fear) into the superior sphere of humanity's common passion, feels the benefit of an elevation of soul; his consciousness is temporarily freed from egotism. (Renouvier, *Introduction à la philosophie analytique de l'Histoire*, p. 354.)

NOTE H
(Page 74)

. . . Napoleon, who ordered the chief of police to take measures for the history of France to be written in a manner favorable to his own throne.

Here are some portions of a note on this subject dictated by Napoleon at Bordeaux in 1808. It promulgates the conception of history as practiced, *mutatis mutandis*, by many of our historians of the past:—

"I do not approve the principles laid down in his note by the Minister of the Interior. They were true twenty years ago, they will be true sixty years hence, but they are not true to-day. Velly is the one fairly detailed author who has written on the

---

[1] This clearly shows in what sense Renouvier is an "individualist." (See above, page 100.)

history of France. The abridged chronology of the President Hénault is a good classical book. It is useful to have them both continued. *It is of the greatest importance to make certain of the spirit in which these continuations are written.* I ordered the Minister of Police to look after the continuation of Millot, and I desire the two Ministers will consult over the continuation of Velly and the President Hénault. . . .

"They are to be just to Henri IV, Louis XIII, Louis XIV and Louis XV, but without adulation. The September Massacres and the horrors of the Revolution must be painted in the same colours as the Inquisition and the massacres of the Sixteen. They must take care to avoid all reaction in speaking of the Revolution, no man could have opposed it successfully. No blame attaches either to those who perished or to those who survived. There was no individual power capable of changing the elements and foreseeing the events which arose from the nature of things and circumstances.

"They are to point out the perpetual disorganization of the national finances, the chaos of the provincial assembles, the claims of the Parlements, the lack of regulation and resort in the administration. This checkered France, without unity of laws and administration, was rather a union of twenty Kingdoms than a single State, so that one breathes freely on coming to the period when the benefits of unity of laws, administration and territory are enjoyed. . . . The opinion expressed by the Minister, which, if followed, would result in abandoning this task to private enterprise and the speculation of some publisher, is wrong and could only produce regrettable results."

Of course, the champions of authority are not the only persons who make history serve their own interests. Condorcet (*Tableau historique*, 10ᵉ Epoque) says that history should serve "to maintain an active vigilance in recognizing and crushing under the weight of Reason the first germs of superstition and tyranny, if they ever dare to appear again.

NOTE I

(Page 81)

Humanitarianism and Humanism.

Here, on this subject, is a curious passage from one of the ancients:—

"Those who created the Latin language and those who spoke it well do not give the word *humanitas* the vulgar meaning which is synonymous with the Greek word *philanthropia*, which means an active kindness, a tender benevolence for all men. But they give the word the meaning which the Greeks attach to *paideia*, which we call education, knowledge of the fine arts. Those who show the most taste and disposition for these studies are the most worthy to be called *humanissimi*. For man alone among all living beings is able to devote himself to cultivating a study which for that reason has been called *humanitas.* Such is the meaning given to this by the ancients, particularly by Varro and Cicero. Almost all their works show examples, so I shall content myself with quoting one only. I have chosen the opening of the first book of Varro 'Concerning human things': 'Praxiteles, qui propter artificium egregium nemini est paulum modo humaniori ignotus (Praxiteles, whose excellent talent as an artist has made him known to every man at all skilled in the arts).' Here *humanior* does not bear the vulgar meaning of easy, tractable, benevolent even though lacking in knowledge of letters. That meaning would not express the author's thought. It means an educated, a learned man, one who is acquainted with Praxiteles through books and history." (*Aulus Gellius, Noctes Atticae,* Book XIII, XVI.)

NOTE J

(Page 104)

. . . *they cannot sufficiently denounce all institutions based on liberty and discussion.*

Note that the novelty here lies in the passion, the fury with which they condemn liberty of discussion. Otherwise, we see most of the so-called liberal thinkers in history themselves recognize the necessity for submission to the sovereign's judgment. Spinoza declares that "there is no possible government if every man makes himself the defender of his own rights and the rights of others." The *Letters of Descartes* contain passages in favor of the "reason of State."

It is perhaps not sufficiently noticed how frequently the old French absolute monarchists say that justice is the chief function of the sovereign. "The most important of the King's rights," says one of these theorists (Guy Coquille, *Institution du droit des Français*, 1608) "is to make *the laws and general statutes for the good order of his Kingdom.*" Another (Loyseau, *Des Seigneuries*, 1608) says: "The usage of public *lordship must be regulated by justice. . . .*" Bossuet (*Instruction à Louis XIV*) says: "When the King administers justice or has it exactly administered in accordance with the laws, *which is his principal function. . . .*" The modern absolute monarchists, even French, seem to be inspired by the German theorist, who says: "The State has two functions to perform: the administration of justice and the waging of war. *But war is by far the principal.*" (Treitschke.)

Note this famous passage from Bossuet (*Pol.*, Book VIII, art. II, par. I):

"It is one thing for it (the government) to be absolute, another for it to be arbitrary. It is absolute in relation to constraint, there being no power which is capable of compelling the sovereign, who in this sense is independent of all human authority. But it does not follow that government is arbitrary; because, apart from the fact that all things are subject to God's judgment (which applies also to the government we have called arbitrary), there are laws in empires, and everything which is done contrary to them is void of right."

It will be seen that the defense of arbitrary government is a new thing among French teachers, even in regard to Bossuet. (I am speaking of Bossuet's *doctrines*, not of his practical advice.)

NOTE K

(Page 116)

This is the teaching of Nietzsche.

I must repeat that throughout this work I am considering the teaching of Nietzsche (and Hegel's too) in so far as it has become the pretext for a great moral preaching, though I know perfectly well that in reality this teaching is something far more complex. I shall quote the following judicious observation, in connection with the fact that certain philosophers have only themselves to blame for "the misunderstanding of their true thought":

"Nietzscheism has been subjected to the same test as Hegelianism. And no doubt here and there philosophical themes have served especially as pretexts to cover up a new offensive on the part of barbarism. *But the fact that they have been utilized, the manner in which they have been utilized, have a significance which must not be overlooked.* Is it not the criterion of a philosophy which may be called rational without reserve and equivocation, that it should remain incorruptibly faithful to itself? On the other hand, *the systems which begin by accepting contradictions, reserving the right to add that they are capable of surmounting them or of 'living' them, lodge their enemy in their midst.* Their punishment is that their antithesis still resembles them; and that is what has happened to Nietzsche." (L. Brunschvicg, *Le Progrès de la Conscience dans la philosophie occidentale*, p. 431.) This book contains an excellent exposition of "Hegelian themes" and "Nietzschean themes," precisely insofar as they have become political breviaries.

NOTE L

(Page 119)

Long before the disciples of Taine and Auguste Comte.

When this book appeared in a periodical, certain persons declared that the whole of my attack on the modern "clerk" went astray because I did not give more space to the author of *Origines de la France Contemporaine.* He, they said, was the "great realist 'clerk' of the past fifty years, while those I attacked were only his small change." (This sudden contempt for the thought of Barrès and Maurras on the part of certain people is certainly surprising.)

There is here a manifest abuse of the word *realism.* Taine threw light on the true nature of the real, or rather the political real, and reminded

230

the universalist that this domain is not under his jurisdiction. He never *exalted* this real at the expense of the universal, which is the realism I am denouncing here. He plainly taught, on the contrary, that the universalist who stays in his own domain (see his admiration for Spinoza and Goethe) is the great human model. Compare this with Maurras for whom the universalist, even when non-political (the infinitist, the pantheist) is profoundly contemptible. It is also difficult for me to see Taine as the godfather of those who glorify the soldier at the expense of the man of justice and the man of study,[1] who exhort the nations to cultivate their prejudices where they are "totally foreign to reason" (Barrès) and who declare that the intelligence which cares nothing about what is social is the activity of a savage. I think Taine would cheerfully say of those who claim to derive from him the same thing that M. Bergson is reported to have said of some of his "disciples": "These gentlemen are most original."

Nevertheless, Taine seems to me to be the initiator of the modern realists in two points. The first is his condemnation of individualism, more exactly, of the moral liberty of the citizen (for this, at bottom, is the meaning of his regret for the old corporations, and, more generally, of his exhortation to form groups, which shape the individual's soul, instead of allowing it to be autonomous as against the State) ; and the second, which is far more novel

[1] See his hymn to the mathematician Franz Woepfke.

than the first among French teachers, is his condemnation of idealist education. The peroration of
the *"Régime moderne"* obviously establishes the
whole educational argument of the *Déracines* and
L'Étape:—

"Sometimes when he is with his intimates, as bit-
ter and as overfatigued as he is, the young man is
tempted to say to us: 'By your education you in-
duced us to believe that the world is made in a
certain way. You deceived us. It is much uglier,
stupider, dirtier, gloomier and harsher, at least to
our sensibility and our imagination. You think
they are over-excited and out of gear; well, if they
are, it is your fault. That is why we curse and
despise the whole of your world, and reject your
pretended truths, which for us are lies, including
those elementary and primary truths which you say
are evident to common sense, and upon which you
build your laws, your institutions, your society,
your philosophy, your sciences and your arts.'
That is what contemporary youth have been telling
us aloud for fifteen years by their tastes, their opinions, their inclinations in literature, the arts and
life."

Against this manifesto in favor of a practical
education, let me set this protest of a true descendant of Montaigne, Pascal and Montesquieu:

"In his diatribe for the classical spirit and the
primary truths of reason and philosophy which direct literary education of all kinds, Taine comes to
use words similar to those of the adversaries of an-

cient literature,[1] of the general ideas which are inseparable from them, and of disinterested culture even. The only object would then be to prepare persons for an empirical world,[2] people taught to know the world as it is, and trained to make it continue as it now is. However, the school laws are too recent for one to be able decently to blame them for the evils of the age, and make them the cause of the hatred and scorn poured on society by those who are bored, enervate and out of their class. However, even if it were true that the comparison between the general principles of reason, morality and beauty, and empirical life engendered more disgust with the realities than it has done in the past, it would be a sad paradox to ask that this danger should be averted by banishing from education all elevated views and all idealism." (Renouvier, *Philosophie analytique de l'Histoire*, tome iv, p. 541.)

Note M
(Page 120)

This cult brings out a silliness of mind which to me seems wholly an acquisition of the nineteenth century.

This silliness of mind assumes another form, i.e. the belief (rigidly formulated by Maurras) that in politics you can find laws of cause and effect as

---

[1] Jules Lemaître was explicitly this adversary.
[2] "For an empirical France," say Barrès and Bourget.

certainly valid as those of weight or electricity. ("Politics are a *science*.") This is the superstition of science, held to be competent in all domains, including that of morality; a superstition which, I repeat, is an acquisition of the nineteenth century. It remains to discover whether those who brandish this doctrine believe in it or whether they simply want to give the prestige of a scientific appearance to the passions of their hearts, which they perfectly well know are nothing but passions. It is to be noted that the dogma that history is obedient to scientific laws is preached especially by partisans of arbitrary authority. This is quite natural, since it eliminates the two realities they most hate, i.e. human liberty and the historical action of the individual.

NOTE N

(Page 124)

Our age has seen priests of the mind teaching that the gregarious is the praiseworthy form of thought, and that independent thought is contemptible.

Note that what is new in this crusade against individualism (the great apostle of which is M. Maurras) is not the recognition that "the individual is only an abstraction," that to a great extent, he is formed by his race, his surroundings, his nation, a thousand things which are not himself. The novelty is the cult for this servitude, the order given to mankind to submit entirely to it, the contempt shown for any attempt to get free from it. Once again this is the cult (so strange in French thinkers) for the *inevitable* part of the human being, the hatred for its free part.

Note that those who to-day preach obedience of the mind, not only demand it from the uncultured masses but from the men of thought, *especially* from the men of thought. The anti-individualists of the Dreyfus affair particularly opposed the independence of scientists, writers, and philosophers —"the mad vanity of a few intellectuals." Nevertheless, the most curious thing is not that they require this obedience, but that they obtain it. When M. Maritain declares that "every one cannot philosophize and that, for men, the essential thing is to choose a master," and when M. Maurras asserts that the function of most minds is to be "servants" and to reflect the thought of some leader, these teachers find a number of men of thought to applaud and abdicate their liberty of mind in their favor. The thinkers of the eighteenth century said: "A religion is needed for the people." Those of our age say: "A religion is needed for ourselves." What Barrès wrote: "The part of the masters is to justify the habits and prejudices of France, so as best to prepare our children to take their place in the national procession," he certainly meant that he and his colleagues were to walk in this procession. Here we again come upon that thirst for discipline which I spoke of above and which seemed to me so worthy of remark in the descendants of Montaigne and Renan. The cause, I said, was their desire to belong to a "strong group." In them it also arises from a feeling for the artistic value of regimenting a collection of men in a beautiful "procession," and also from the joy felt by so many souls in being governed, if not having to make the effort to think for themselves—a most curious joy in so-called men of thought.

The cult for the collective soul, with all its violation of human consciousness, seems to me admirably denounced by a passage of Maine de Biran, quoted by M. L. Brunschvicg (op. cit., *La Sociologie de l'ordre*, p. 526) :—

". . . According to M. Bonald, it is not the human mind, it is not the individual understanding which is the seat, the true subject of inherence of the nations or (universal) truths under discussion; but it is society, which, gifted with a kind of collective understanding different from that of individuals, was from its origin imbued with them through the gift of speech and by virtue of a miraculous influence exerted on the mass alone, independent of its parts. The individual, the man, is nothing; society alone exists; society is the soul of the moral world, it alone exists, while individual persons are only phenomena. Let those who can, understand this social metaphysics. If the author himself understands it clearly, then I am in the wrong. Then we must cease to talk of philosophy and recognize the nothingness of the science of intellectual and moral man, we must admit that all psychology based on the primitive fact of consciousness is simply false, and we must consider science itself as an illusion which perpetually deceives and misleads us by showing us everything, even our own existence, in a false and fantastic light."

M. Brunschvicg very rightly adds: "The antithesis could not be stated more clearly. Either the primary fact of consciousness, or the primary fact of language; either Socrates or Bonald."

Either Socrates or Bonald. Barrès and Maurras made their choice.

NOTE O

(Page 147)

. . . *Péguy who admires philosophies to the extent that "they are good fighters."* [1]

This determination to praise philosophers for their virtues of action rather than for their intellectual virtues is very frequent among men of thought to-day. In his *Souvenirs concernant Lagneau*, Alain, wishing to give as favorable a picture of his master as possible, praises his energy and his resolution at least as much as his intelligence. It is also very remarkable—although here literature only is in question—to see a professor of moral

---

[1] "Note sur M. Bergson et la philosophie bergsonienne," Cahiers de la Quinzaine. See my book, *Sur le Succès du Bergsonisme*, page 158.

science (M. Jacques Bardoux) setting a special value on those French literary men who were soldiers, i.e. Vauvenargues, Vigny, Péguy. As to the men of letters themselves, I shall content myself with pointing out that one of them who is most applauded by his own colleagues recently declared that he chiefly admired d'Annunzio for his attitude as an officer, and expressed regret that he had returned to literature.[1] The Emperor Julian praised Aristotle for having said that he felt prouder of being the author of his *Treatise on Theology* than he would have felt if he had destroyed the power of the Persians. One might still find soldiers in France who would agree with this judgment, but very few men of letters. Elsewhere (*Les Sentiments de Critias*, p. 206) I have attempted to give the history and the explanation of this desire (so curious in men of the pen) to exalt a warlike life and to scorn a sedentary life. Note that this characteristic is to be seen in contemporary

[1] The same thing is to be found in Lamartine when he says of Byron: "There is more true, imperishable poetry in the tent at Missolonghi where he lies prostrate with fever, under arms, than in all his works." (*Commentaire de la 2e Meditation.*) This is precisely the teaching adopted by Barrès, Suarès, Péguy (the last preached it by his example, however), which comes down to saying: "There is more poetry in a heroic death than in all the activities of the mind." Note that this position is by no means common to all the Romantics. Hugo, Vigny, Michelet, felt all the poetry of action, but they never appear to think it superior to the poetry of the lofty forms of intellectual life. Hugo never thought of sacrificing Homer or Galilei to Napoleon, or even to Hoche—to take a disinterested hero such as Lamartine praises in Byron.

writers long before the war of 1914, and that those who talk most about a warlike life are not always those who lead it.

The new thing, I repeat, is not that we see men of letters praising an active life and scorning a sedentary life; it is *the absence of naïveté, the dogmatic tone.* When Ronsard exclaims: "Good Gods, who would praise those who let life go by bent over books" [1]; when Bertrand de Born wishes that "no man of high lineage should have any thought but cutting off heads and arms"; when Froissart sings the glories of chivalry and casts his scorn in the faces of the bourgeois, no one will take these candid lyre-players, who like noble poses and do not even know that the word doctrine exists, for the ancestors of our grave professors of belligerent esthetics. Moreover, I doubt whether the author of *Scenes and Doctrines of Nationalism* would have condescended to be a descendant of these simple-minded persons.

I find scorn for the life of the mind clearly professed in a dogmatic tone, in a writer of the seventeenth century who frequently reminds one of certain modern authors by his efforts to humiliate the toga before the sword. (It is true that this writer was a gentleman of the very minor nobility.)

"Certainly, there is no better way of relaxing the vigor of men's courage than to occupy their minds with peaceful and sedentary exercises and

[1] Note that Ronsard is the very type of the man "bent over books."

idleness cannot enter civilized States in a more subtle or dangerous disguise than that of literature. Lazy and idle persons have in part ruined commerce and agriculture, which are the cause of the weakness of our condition and the cowardice of our age." (J. L. de Balzac, *Le Prince*, 1631. He then admits literature and the sciences to the State insofar (as "they strengthen and embellish the Mother-country.")

On the other hand, a master from the great period of French literature writes a eulogy of the life of the mind at the expense of the active mind, which I hardly think would be accepted by many of the moderns who venerate that period (I am especially thinking of those who admire the thought of Georges Sorel).

"In France great strength of character and width of mind are needed if a man is to reject offices and employments and thus consent to remain at home and do nothing. Scarcely any one possesses sufficient merit to play this part with dignity, nor sufficient resources to fill up the void of time without what the vulgar call 'business.' But the wise man's idleness needs only a better name, and we ought to say that one who meditates, talks, reads and is calm, is working." (La Bruyère, *Du Mérite personnel.*)

NOTE P

(Page 153)

The "Manifesto of the Party of Intelligence"
(*Figaro, 19th July, 1919*).

This manifesto, signed by fifty-four French
writers, several of whom are among the teachers
most respected by their fellow-citizens, is of the
greatest importance to the present inquiry. In
addition to the strange passage on the Church's
mission which I quoted above, it contains things
like this:—

"Nationalism, which the conceptions of the intelligence impose on political conduct as well as on
the order of the world, is a reasonable, humane
system, and French in addition."
And further on:—

"When a literature becomes national does it not
acquire a more universal significance, a more hu-
manly general interest?"
And again:—

"We believe—and the world believes with us—
that it is part of the destiny of our race to defend
the spiritual interests of humanity. . . . We are
solicitous for Europe and all the humanity remaining in the world. French humanity is the sovereign
protector of this."
And above all:—

"Victorious France means to take her place again

in the order of the mind, the only order whereby a legitimate domination may be exercised."

Hence the desire to found (the manifesto itself underlines the words) : *"The intellectual Federation of Europe and the world under the aegis of victorious France, the guardian of civilization."*

Victory under arms conferring the right to command in the intellectual order—that is professed to-day by French thinkers! One remembers the Roman writers, from whom these thinkers claim descent, who took as the leader of their minds Greece, which had been conquered by force of arms; one also remembers the German teachers of 1871 who also claimed intellectual hegemony for their "victorious" nation, which they too claimed as "the guardian of civilization."[1]

When this manifesto was published, somewhat similar reflections seem to have occurred to the mind of one of our great writers. In a letter concerning this document,[2] Marcel Proust deplores the proclamation of "a kind of 'Frankreich ueber alles,' the policeman of the literature of all nations." As a true priest of the mind, he goes on: "Why take this peremptory attitude towards other countries in such matters as literature, where a man only reigns by persuasion?" I am happy to take this

[1] "Germany is the protector and the support of European civilization." (Lamprecht.) "After the war Germany will again take up her historic task, which is to be the heart of Europe and to prepare European humanity." (Wilhelm II, *Temps*, 14th September, 1915.)

[2] See Robert Dreyfus, *Souvenirs sur Marcel Proust*, page 336.

opportunity to do homage to this true "clerk," and to say that I know that there are still other writers in France beside those who only believe in the virtue of cold steel.

NOTE Q

(Page 171)

Those who base their judgments on their artistic sensibilities.

This artistic origin of the political attitudes of so many men of letters has been pointed out with great ability by M. Daniel Halévy in the case of M. Maurras. In an old article (*La Grande France,* 1902) M. Halévy quotes this beautiful passage from M. Maurras's *Anthinéa* on the walk of women carrying a clay pot balanced on their heads:—
"The bosom swells and is modeled like a vase, it opens like a flower. The neck settles, the loins strain nervously. Their walk becomes graver and more supple, is measured with an inestimable sobriety; it unrolls in the mind like a piece of music. This living pillar moves, glides, advances, without being interrupted by any sudden jerk or any break. It follows the undulations of the ground, adapts itself to the slightest rises, and thus resembles the stem of a beautiful young tree set free from its roots, moving over the ground without leaving it for a fraction of an inch. An infinite multitude of half-pauses make the jerks imperceptible, or one is only conscious of their succession, a continual

243

harmony which leaves its curves in the air. . . ."

M. Daniel Halévy adds:—

"I quote the whole passage because it gives the very idea of Charles Maurras. For his classical way of thought, things are beautiful, not from the shocks of feeling and passion, but from the form and rhythm which give them continuity, or rather existence in the human sense of the word. M. Charles Maurras applies this taste for form to the study of history, and that is the whole of his 'sociology.'"

There could be no better definition of the type of man for whom things are good insofar as they satisfy his artistic sensibility. Let me place in opposition to him the exactly contrary type, leaving the reader to judge which of the two may claim to belong to "the intelligence":—

". . . For the perfection of things should be measured by their nature alone, and things are not more or less perfect because they flatter or wound our senses." (Spinoza.)

Lightning Source UK Ltd.
Milton Keynes UK
UKOW05f1819090114

224306UK00001B/93/P